# WOODEN PUZZLES

# WOODEN PUZZLES

## 20 Handmade Puzzles and Brain Teasers

BRIAN MENOLD

The Taunton Press

Text © 2016 by Brian Menold
Photographs © 2016 by The Taunton Press, Inc.
Illustrations © 2016 by The Taunton Press, Inc.
All rights reserved.

The Taunton Press, Inc.
63 South Main Street
PO Box 5506
Newtown, CT 06470-5506
e-mail: tp@taunton.com

Editors: Peter Chapman, Christina Glennon
Copy editor: Diane Sinitsky
Jacket/Cover design: Stacy Wakefield Forte
Interior design: Rosalind Loeb Wanke, Lynne Phillips
Layout: Stacy Wakefield Forte
Illustrator: Mario Ferro
Photographer: Brian Menold, except for the photos on pp. 2, 3, 32, 36, 43, 48, 54, 60, 64, 67, 71, 74, 80, 86, 93, 96, 99,
          104, 108, 114, 119, 125, and 128 by Scott Phillips
Cover photographer: Scott Phillips, except for the photos on the bottom of the back cover by Brian Menold

The following names/manufacturers appearing in *Wooden Puzzles* are trademarks: Lego®; Plexiglas®; Tinkertoy®;
Titebond® III; X-Acto®

Library of Congress Cataloging-in-Publication Data

Names: Menold, Brian, author.
Title: Wooden puzzles : 20 handmade puzzles and brain teasers / Brian Menold.
Description: Newtown, CT : The Taunton Press, Inc., [2016]
Identifiers: LCCN 2016027747 | ISBN 9781631863608
Subjects: LCSH: Wooden toy making. | Woodwork–Patterns | Puzzles.
Classification: LCC TT174.5.W6 M46 2016 | DDC 745.592–dc23
LC record available at https://lccn.loc.gov/2016027747

Printed in the United States of America
10 9 8 7 6 5 4 3 2 1

## DEDICATION

*To Denise*

## ABOUT YOUR SAFETY

Working wood is inherently dangerous. Using hand or power tools improperly or ignoring safety
practices can lead to permanent injury or even death. Don't try to perform operations you learn
about here (or elsewhere) unless you're certain they are safe for you. If something about an
operation doesn't feel right, don't do it. Look for another way. We want you to enjoy the craft,
so please keep safety foremost in your mind whenever you're in the shop.

# Acknowledgments

When I decided to write this book, I have to admit that I was a little intimidated about undertaking such a daunting task. I had never attempted anything like this before, and writing seemed like such a solitary pursuit. So I was very uncertain about the prospect of completing such an overwhelming job on my own.

Shortly after I began, I realized I was not on my own at all. There was an entire community of woodworkers, puzzle designers, and puzzle collectors who have shaped my world the past several years. I owe all of these people a great deal of gratitude. But more specifically, I would never have been able to complete this book, or even make puzzle making my vocation, if it were not for the clever designers whose puzzles are featured in this book. I would especially like to thank Stewart T. Coffin. Stewart was the inspiration for the making of my first wooden puzzle. His brilliant designs, excellent craftsmanship, and numerous publications have influenced many puzzle makers and designers. His creativity, kindness, and generosity have earned him respect and admiration throughout the puzzle community.

Above all else, I thank my wife, Denise. Her support and encouragement throughout this project made the job so much easier. The strength that she exhibits each and every day kept me going to the very last puzzle.

# Contents

# Introduction

I have two vivid memories from my childhood: spending hours sitting at the kitchen table putting together plastic models and enjoying time in my father's workshop. While I can't ever remember my dad actually making anything in that shop, I have heard several family stories of projects gone awry. You see, while my father managed to accumulate a large number of tools, he wasn't a very handy guy. His basement shop consisted of an expansive bench with many small drawers, hidden shelves, hanging tools, and

secret nooks. It was his love of tools and this small basement workshop he kept that provided me with the opportunity to spend many hours making small projects and exploring the many drawers and cubbies that his workshop held. This early introduction to woodworking, along with the enjoyment of assembling those plastic models, was probably the basis for my passion for making wooden puzzles.

Woodworking has been in my blood for most of my life. I have been nailing bits of wood together since I was a young boy. My parents even allowed me to remodel my bedroom as a teenager, adding shelves, trim, and built-in furniture. My first home was a "handyman special." That led to a decision my wife and I made, which was to build our own home—the first, and certainly the largest, puzzle I ever built! A geodesic dome design, it was a precursor to some of the intricate shapes I create from wood today.

In this book, I present a number of basic puzzle designs. Like most of the puzzles I make, these designs were found online and the plans provided to me by the designers. This does not mean they are easy or geared for young children. On the contrary, most of the puzzles in this book will baffle many adults. Much of the appeal of a puzzle is in the solver's perception that he or she can master it easily. That perception comes from the first impression you get when looking at a puzzle. You might say, "It's only a few pieces and they are large, simple shapes. It can't be that difficult." That's when the frustration begins! But that same perception, that it must be easy, is what keeps someone interested enough to fight through the frustration to try to solve it.

One misconception about puzzles is that they are mainly for children. As I have gotten further into the world of puzzles, I have found that many collectors are college professors, scientists, mathematicians, and engineers. They are part of a large international community of collectors, and they take their puzzle collecting very seriously. Some have built rooms in their homes that are dedicated to the display of their collections. I have come to appreciate the love they have for this hobby and have even become a bit of a collector myself. Although I rarely have the opportunity to make myself a copy of a favorite puzzle, I usually keep a copy of every puzzle I make.

Even though I began this journey as a woodworker and not a puzzle enthusiast, my interest in the puzzles themselves has grown over the years. I have found that my interest in making a puzzle diminishes greatly after the first one is completed, a condition I must constantly overcome. Production runs of a dozen or more of the same puzzle are essential to achieve any level of efficiency. Since I make my living making and selling puzzles, efficiency is critical. But I still find myself getting most of my satisfaction from making a prototype, playing with it, and refining the details before production begins. As much as I love woodworking, it sometimes takes a back seat to the enjoyment I get from working on a new puzzle.

Exploring the world of puzzles is an unending journey. We often tend to think, "Everything has been done already." Not true! New designs are being developed every day. My friend Ken Irvine created the Little Kenny design specifically for this book. Dozens of new designs are produced every day, which will provide you with an endless supply of fresh ideas. (It's important to note that all puzzle designs are the property of the designer. I always seek permission from a designer before producing any copies to sell.)

I invite you to explore the world of puzzle making. I have found it to be both a rewarding hobby and an enjoyable vocation. Start with something small and easy, such as the Five-Piece Solid Block design. When you see the pleasure your projects bring to puzzle enthusiasts of all ages, you may find yourself pursuing your new passion: making puzzles.

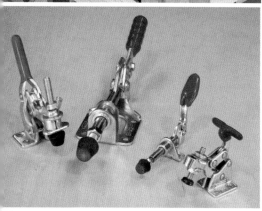

# GETTING STARTED

# TOOLS FOR PUZZLE MAKING

Most of the projects in this book do not require a professionally outfitted shop. On the contrary, my shop contains a 30-year-old contractor tablesaw and a 12-in. bandsaw; the rest of my tools are all essentially benchtop models. We tend to think that you must have the latest and greatest tools to turn out professional, top-quality pieces, but it is much more important to understand the capability of the tools you own and keep them maintained and calibrated properly. Don't get me wrong, I long for the day when I can upgrade my next tool, but until I do, I will make the most of the tools I have, and

**The author's** puzzle-making workshop.

turn out products that are sought out by collectors all over the world.

The only limitation I would suggest to you as a woodworker is that if you are a hand tools–only woodworker, puzzle making may not be for you. While we have all seen woodworkers turn out some amazing projects using only a minimum of hand tools, most of these puzzle designs require a level of precision that can challenge you even using finely tuned power tools. I do use chisels occasionally for taking apart errantly glued pieces or a small handsaw for trimming pieces left intentionally long, but that's about it. And my handplanes have never been used in puzzle making. Achieving the necessary level of precision with a handplane is not practical unless you are only interested in making non-interlocking puzzles.

# A Basic Set of Tools

I have known craftsmen who have made some wonderful puzzles with little more than a chopsaw and a few sheets of sandpaper, but that is the exception rather than the rule. The list of tools that I recommend here has been drawn from what I have in my shop today. Like all woodworking operations, my methods are not the only way to make puzzles. It is simply what works for me in my shop. And because I make puzzles for a living, I am often looking for the most efficient way to perform a task. If you are making puzzles for personal enjoyment, some of these tools or procedures may not appeal to you. Regardless of your reasons for making puzzles, it can and should be an enjoyable hobby. So adapt these recommendations to what suits your shop and skills.

### TABLESAW

The tablesaw is the workhorse of most workshops, and mine is no exception. To get the accuracy needed to make quality puzzles, I rely heavily on my tablesaw and use it not only to

## A BASIC LIST OF TOOLS FOR PUZZLE MAKING

- Tablesaw
- Planer
- Jointer
- Disk/belt sander
- Drill press
- Measuring tools
- Clamps
- Sanding tools (finish sanding)
- Finishing supplies (not required but suggested)

make finished, precise cuts of pieces but also to mill stock. When using my tablesaw, I regularly use jigs for most operations. Consistency and efficiency are the driving force behind this. With my tablesaw, I strive to get finished pieces

off the saw. Sanding is generally reserved for getting the pieces ready for finish.

### TABLESAW BLADES

I cannot emphasize enough the need for high-quality, sharp blades. In my early years of woodworking, I went the route of buying anything to get by as cheaply as possible, which proved more costly in the long run. High-quality blades stay sharp longer, have a longer life span, and are sharper right out of the box. I recommend that you invest in both a good crosscut blade (80 teeth per inch [TPI]) and a rip blade (20 to 24 TPI). This is one area where efficiency may seem to go out the window because switching blades frequently can be time-consuming. I change blades throughout the day depending on the operation I am performing. You do not have to change that often though, because when cutting pieces, you are usually making all your rip cuts first, then making all the crosscuts at one time. Once again, this is a personal preference. I

**A tablesaw** (shown here with a crosscutting jig) is an essential tool for puzzle making.

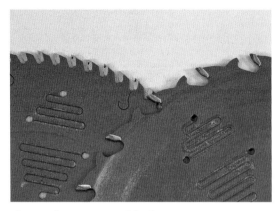

**The author's go-to blades** for puzzle making are an 80-TPI crosscut blade (left) and a 24-TPI rip blade (right).

involves cutting many small pieces. Do the math. If you are cutting cubes that are ⅝ in., a full-kerf blade will result in 10% more waste—after you have already wasted about 15% of your stock milling it to size! A thin-kerf blade can reduce that significantly. And when working with exotic woods that cost $20 to $80 per board foot, it can make quite a difference.

### PLANER

One of the benefits of puzzle making is that you don't need large, high-powered, expensive tools. Almost everything you do after the initial milling of stock is done on a small scale. I use a typical benchtop planer, but if you don't have a planer, you can readily purchase stock in manageable, premilled sizes. Just remember to choose your stock carefully.

### JOINTER

A jointer is essential for flattening and squaring up your stock. I have a 4-in. jointer that has served me well for more than 10 years, although it's a bit on the small side (and will be the next upgrade to my shop). At only 4 in., I must rip my stock down to 4 in. or less to flatten it and square one edge before planing it to the proper thickness. As you will see, puzzles often use very little wood, so my 4-in. jointer is sufficient.

have never been happy with the quality of cut I achieve with a general-purpose blade, even if it's a high-quality blade (40 to 60 TPI). I feel you are compromising on both ends.

I also buy only thin-kerf blades. There are two reasons for this. First, my saw is not a powerful cabinet saw that can plow through 8/4 hard maple easily. More important, puzzle making

**TIP**

**Although I get great results** and accurate pieces straight out of my planer, I use a drum sander to remove the milling marks and bring the pieces to final thickness. A drum sander is not an essential tool, but it cuts down on some of the finish sanding later in the process.

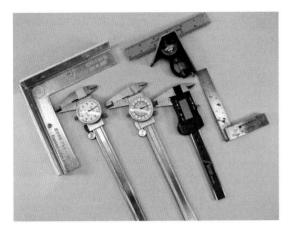

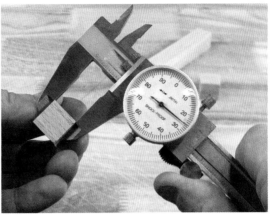

**You'll need a variety** of squares, calipers, and other measuring tools. The author's favorites are the dial calipers on the left and the engineer's square on the right.

**Using dial calipers** enables you to check that your stock is within a few thousandths of the desired measurement, in this case ⅝ in. (0.625 in.).

## DISK/BELT SANDER

My 6-in. disk/4-in. belt sander was a perfect solution for me when I purchased it several years ago. This tool is also on my upgrade list, but with the proper jigs it can definitely do the job. The biggest challenge with a smaller tool like mine is poor dust collection, an important consideration as puzzle making can generate a lot of dust.

## DRILL PRESS

While a drill press is not an essential tool for puzzle making, the ability to drill perfectly straight, 90° holes can be essential for some designs, as in the case of the Peg Pile puzzle (see pp. 118–123). Otherwise, it is one of the lesser-used tools in my shop. As a matter of fact, it gets more use as a sanding tool when I insert a sanding mop into the drill press for finishing off some irregularly shaped pieces.

## MEASUREMENT TOOLS

The tools you use for measuring will likely be dictated by what you already own, but if you want to upgrade or purchase some new tools, this is a good place to start. I would highly recommend a good pair of dial calipers that measure to 1/1,000th of an inch. This degree of accuracy may seem like overkill, but once you start making a few puzzles that require a precise fit, you will really appreciate this tool.

I also recommend purchasing set-up blocks or gauges, which are invaluable for quickly and precisely setting up your jigs for cutting parts. And since many puzzles use the same-size pieces, you'll quickly find yourself looking for a convenient spot near the tablesaw for your set. Set-up blocks are available in both decimal and fractional versions. I can no longer process the

**Several tool options** are available to help you accurately set up your jigs. Set-up blocks or gauges come in both fractional and decimal versions.

**Spring clamps** (top) and the blue quick-grip mini-bar clamps (bottom left) see a lot of use in puzzle making. A larger bar clamp (bottom right) also comes in handy for jig making.

**A variety of sanding** options are available. The author keeps several sanding mops, abrasive pads, and sanding sticks close at hand. Shop-made sanding sticks, like the one in the upper right, also come in handy.

addition and subtraction of complex fractions quickly, so I prefer working with decimals. If I need to multiply several fractions, I would rely on my calculator and must convert it to decimals first anyway.

A good square and a ruler, staples in most shops already, round out the essentials for measuring. I also use a few glue-up squares on occasion. These are nice to have, but I would not consider them a necessity.

### CLAMPS

Clamps are just as necessary in puzzle making as they are in any other woodworking process. And as every woodworker knows, you can never have enough. The good part about the clamps for puzzle making is that most of them will fit neatly in a drawer.

The two types of clamps that I use most frequently are spring clamps and quick-grip mini-bar clamps. Spring clamps are inexpensive and fast and easy to use; they are what I rely on most of the time. The one drawback I have experienced is that the padding on the clamp ends leaves marks on some woods. Final sanding usually gets rid of the marks, though they can be

difficult to remove from certain exotic woods. It's also helpful to have a few 12-in. to 24-in. bar clamps when making your jigs, though these larger clamps are rarely required in puzzle making.

### SANDING TOOLS

As I mentioned previously, I use a sanding mop in my drill press. It's a useful tool for small irregularly shaped pieces, and I keep several grits in my shop, relying mostly on fine-grit sanding mops. The 220-grit mop gets most of the action for relieving the edges of parts or getting into those hard-to-reach places. And I never use anything coarser than a 180-grit sanding mop, especially when the mop is new. New sanding mops can be very aggressive, and I recommend breaking them in on some other project or on the edges of a piece that is meant to be rounded over. Occasionally, I will use the sanding mop to smooth out a flat surface. This can also help wear down the mop so that it is not as abrasive and damaging to finer pieces.

It goes without saying that you will also need a variety of grits of sandpaper. While I try to limit the sanding I do to surface prep for finishing, I

Using a sanding mop in a drill press is a great way to sand irregularly shaped pieces. Fine-grit sanding mops are less aggressive and, consequently, safer for delicate pieces.

still occasionally use 120- or 150-grit sandpaper when working on pieces that are not dimensionally critical. I also keep an assortment of sanding sticks, both purchased and homemade, and several different abrasive pads on hand.

## FINISHING SUPPLIES

My finish of choice for wooden puzzles has always been spray lacquer, mainly because of its rapid drying time. And I spray it because of the multiple surfaces of the pieces I am finishing. I have also turned to shellac on occasion. The drying time for shellac is quick, just as for lacquer, and the fumes are not quite as bad, although precautions still need to be taken with all finishing. On occasion, I have also used boiled linseed oil for finishing puzzles. The biggest objection to this finish is the extended drying time. But when time permits, boiled linseed oil can provide nice results with a smooth, soft feel rather than the shiny plastic look of lacquer.

The final step for all puzzles is applying a good coat of wax. Any paste wax will do, but I prefer a microcrystalline wax/polish. It imparts a

**TIP**

**Lacquer fumes** can be harmful, and lacquer should only be used in a well-ventilated area. You must also take the additional safety precautions of wearing the proper respirator and gloves.

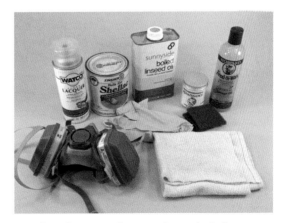

**Finishes for wooden** puzzles include lacquer (the author's favorite), shellac, boiled linseed oil, and wax. Some puzzles receive only a coating of wax. Whatever the finish, be sure to wear an approved respirator and gloves.

**Miscellaneous items** that you might need for puzzle making include everything from tweezers to business cards.

- Tweezers are sometimes needed for placing small parts accurately in small spaces.

- Business cards make great spacers or shims when you need to add several thousandths of an inch.

- Zip-top storage bags are great for holding small parts, especially when making larger quantities of puzzles.

- A chisel is needed to separate mistakes (yes, it will happen!) before the glue has fully dried.

- The little red, black, and blue cubes shown in the photo at left are a tool I purchased online for making prototype puzzles. These are helpful for checking that you have everything right before cutting into your precious wood. They are sold in small sets as "Live Cubes." Snapping together like Legos®, they allow you to make a puzzle and try it out first before making a large batch of something that turns out to be uninteresting.

- Last but not least, blue painter's tape. Anything not covered above can be solved with blue painter's tape!

nice, soft sheen and is gently buffed out immediately after application, speeding up the finishing process.

## MISCELLANEOUS SUPPLIES

Rounding out the list of essentials are the miscellaneous doodads that seem to find their way into every shop. Many of these items would not normally be associated with puzzle making, so I feel the need to mention them here.

- Small glue bottles help keep glue at your fingertips in a neat, manageable, and convenient size.

- An X-Acto® or similar knife is handy for removing excess glue.

- Bamboo skewers are useful for spreading glue in tight spots, and I have used them as dowels to reinforce joints of some puzzles.

- Hobby paintbrushes can get into tight corners with glue or finish.

No matter what tools you have available to you, it will always feel as though you don't have enough. That means you are a normal woodworker. But I hope that you will find that you can make puzzles with a minimum number of tools and that you don't need to have an expansive shop with the latest and greatest of every tool on the market. I made puzzle making into my hobby years ago in my basement shop. It was 10 ft. x 11 ft. and contained two hot-water heaters. My tablesaw and disk/belt sander were the first tools I had when I started. Like every aspect of woodworking, I learned as I went along, and a book like this was my first introduction to the world of puzzle making. I hope this is the beginning of a new hobby for you, too!

# SELECTING WOOD FOR YOUR PUZZLES

Choosing which wood to make your puzzle from is like trying to decide on a paint color for a project. There are many choices, and some are stunning while others will not excite you. But choosing the right wood can turn your puzzle into a work of art.

For the purpose of this book, we will be working with commonly found domestic hardwoods. These woods are readily available at your lumber supplier and in some big-box stores. While red oak is not the best for dimensional stability, I have always found it to be an excellent wood for making puzzles. It is inexpensive, easy to work with, and easy to find and can be purchased S4S (surfaced four sides) almost anywhere you buy lumber. Red oak also glues well and, as a hardwood, is very durable for a puzzle that will probably see a lot of playing time. (If you are making a puzzle for a child, durability is probably a little more important than beauty.) The one drawback to red oak is that is has no distinguish-

**Premilled stock** in standard dimensions suitable for puzzle making is readily available from lumber suppliers and some big-box stores.

## DIMENSIONAL STABILITY

When choosing woods for your puzzles, one of the main considerations is dimensional stability, especially if you live in an area where humidity fluctuates seasonally. Hardwoods are your best option. Grain direction can also play a part in the puzzle's stability, just as it would in any woodworking project. Apply the same principles to puzzle making that you would to any woodworking project. A puzzle that seems tight in humid conditions may be loose and appear sloppily made in a drier area. This is why exotic hardwoods, which may not be as susceptible to these conditions, are often used in puzzle making. Just remember that the scale of these projects means that they do not warrant extreme measures to control the problem.

**TIP**

**If you acquire wood** from furniture or other discarded material, check it with a moisture meter and allow it to acclimate to your shop before milling. Any material that shows signs of warping should not be used.

ing grain pattern. Compared with most other woods, it is pretty ordinary but still serviceable. Two other good choices that will not break the bank are maple and cherry.

While I don't recommend using softwoods for your puzzles, it is a good idea to use pine or whatever you have on hand to make a prototype of any puzzle that you feel may be challenging. Scrap wood is perfect for this, and it is much better to work out any challenges on something from your offcut pile than that nice piece of walnut you purchased for the job. Even some excess 2x4s that are lying around the shop can be used for this purpose.

Another material I have seen used for puzzle making is plywood. Personally, I don't like the look that you get from a puzzle made from plywood. With the right design, you could use the end grain to give an accent to a puzzle, but I find that plywood is more difficult to work with and finish than a nicer hardwood. In spite of its dimensional stability, I recommend staying away from plywood for aesthetic reasons.

## What to Look For

One of the best things about making puzzles is that they don't require a lot of lumber. When you have two dozen or more parts going into a

**A stack of domestic** and exotic wood is ready for puzzle making in the author's shop.

**Resawing** 4/4 or 5/4 stock on a bandsaw allows you to double your yield from a board. Pieces as thin as ¼ in. (right) can be used for some puzzles in this book.

finished product that is only a few inches square, the pieces are usually all fairly small. The downside is that there tends to be much more waste as a percentage of the wood you are cutting. Cutting multiple ¾-in. pieces from a stick of wood with a ⅛-in. kerf on your blade will result in almost ⅟₇ of the wood ending up in your dust-collection system. That is exclusive of the milling process necessary to arrive at the ¾-in. x ¾-in. stock you are cutting. Add in some allowance for bad cuts, possible snipe from the milling process, and checked ends that must be removed, and you have quite a bit of wood that winds up on the shop floor. Keep this in mind before spending $25 or more per board foot for exotic woods.

Later in this book, I'll show you how to make the most of your puzzle by adding elegant touches that really make a piece stand out. And of course, there are exotic woods that you will see throughout the book to whet your appetite when you decide to take puzzle making to the next level. But again, for your first few puzzles, I recommend sticking with what is either easy to pick up locally or perhaps is sitting in your scrap bin.

When shopping for wood, you are most likely going to find ¾-in. stock, in varying widths, at the big-box stores. This is a great place to start. You can pick up enough ¾-in. red oak for just a few dollars to make yourself three or four puzzles.

If you buy your lumber from a lumberyard or specialty wood distributor, you may have other options. I frequently purchase some of the lumber I use as 4/4 or 5/4 rough stock. If I happen to be making puzzles that require ⅝-in. or even ½-in. stock, I can resaw the material and double my yield from the board. If I purchase 5/4 stock for a particular puzzle, I will often resaw ¼ in. off the boards to be used for future puzzles. After the resawing, I can mill the remaining piece to ¾ in. or ⅝ in., which is another size that is frequently used.

One other feature to bear in mind when shopping for wood is grain. At least when beginning puzzle making, you should look for straight-grain woods. Beautifully figured grain is appealing, but it can be tricky to work with, especially when you're cutting very small pieces. It can also present challenges when cutting longer strips of

**Shown here** are a few examples of exotic woods (and some domestic woods) that are readily available. Combining two or more woods in a puzzle can create some amazing results.

wood for puzzles that require them. Any twist or bend in the wood may prevent you from properly gluing up the puzzle (or the puzzle from working at all). This is another reason why I recommend starting out with red oak. It is relatively straight grained and properly dried so that it doesn't twist or warp. Save the more exotic stuff until you feel more comfortable tackling a fancier puzzle.

## Salvaged Wood

Wood for your puzzles can come from many places. One great source I've found is discarded furniture. You are working with small pieces, and unwanted furniture can be a good resource. A few years back, I salvaged a dresser from a neighbor, and taking apart the drawers yielded some ¼-in. mahogany that I used to make dozens of puzzles. A set of drawers from another dresser provided me with some interesting poplar. I don't often use poplar, but it does occasion-

ally have some unique colors. These particular pieces were a nice shade of green, and I used them for some leaves that adorned the top of a puzzle frame. Quite a find! So keep your eyes open for opportunities. Unlike building furniture, which can require a pickup truck to get your material home, found puzzle supplies can sometimes be carried under one arm.

When salvaging material, I don't recommend using green wood or any wood that has not completely dried. In other words, that nice piece of wood you found in your stack of firewood will probably not make a great puzzle. Warping, twisting, or cupping can render any puzzle unusable or at the very least unattractive. I suggest you buy your wood only from reputable suppliers or sources you are familiar with. I have managed to find some nice wood in pallets—including maple, red and white oak, and even walnut. If you go this route, you must exercise caution and know the source of the pallets to verify that the wood is safe to use.

## Using Exotic Woods

Once you've advanced your puzzle-making skills, I strongly recommend you try some more exotic species of woods. The grain and colors available are absolutely stunning. Combining grain patterns and colors can result in some visually impressive puzzles. Most of the puzzle collectors who are my customers will only buy puzzles made from these exotic woods. Thoughtful planning can help minimize the expense of these purchases by combining the less expensive domestic species with accents from the exotic woods. You'll find more on this in "Taking Your Puzzles to the Next Level" (see p. 134).

Something to keep in mind when working with exotic wood species: What you see isn't always what you get. Choosing exotic wood for its grain and color can be a challenge when looking at rough stock. Most lumber dealers frown upon your bringing a plane to shave off some wood to better see the color and grain pattern of a board. That said, I do have one supplier who displays several boards of each species that are surfaced on both sides and prices it the same as the other rough boards. If I am only purchasing one board, I can easily decide which to choose as the beauty of the wood is in full view. If I need more than one, I am relatively certain that the others will be as good as the planed piece.

One more shortcoming of many exotic woods is their tendency to fade or change color over time. Many of the vivid hues that you see when you first mill your stock fade or darken over time. In much the same way that cherry attains a deep, rich reddish-brown tone that is very desirable, exotic woods often turn brown or even black over time. This change in color is hastened by exposure to sunlight, and there is little that can be done to stop it. Just bear this in mind when planning your project. All species undergo this change over differing amounts of time. Lignum vitae (shown above right ) is one of the quickest to change, whereas Yellowheart does a

**Some exotic woods** have a tendency to change color over time, as exhibited dramatically by the lignum vitae boards shown here.

fairly good job of maintaining its bright yellow color. Darker woods, like wenge, don't change much over time either.

## Puzzle Sizes

When we talk about puzzle sizes, generally we are referring to the overall finished size of the puzzle. However, during construction, we often need to refer to the unit size of a single piece. For example, the Five-Piece Solid Block puzzle (see p. 36) is a 3 x 3 x 3 cube that is made from twenty-seven ³⁄₄-in. cubes, giving it a final dimension of 2¼ in. x 2¼ in. x 2¼ in. As puzzle designs get larger (many consist of six to eight units across), we need to scale down the thickness of the wood used or else you would wind up with a puzzle that is 6 in. square. A puzzle this size would not only require quite a bit of stock, but it would also be unwieldy and awkward to play with.

The table on p. 35 gives some guidelines for stock sizes when shopping for lumber for a particular puzzle. Don't forget to factor in 25% to 30% waste factor when getting started. If you're making a puzzle with a larger number of units, you will be planing off a significant amount of wood or resawing. Keep this in mind and don't overbuy—or adjust the size of your puzzle.

# JIGS FOR PUZZLE MAKING

I strongly recommend the use of jigs in puzzle making. While many of the operations these jigs perform can be accomplished without them, you will find that the time savings far outweigh the inconvenience of spending the extra time making a jig. More important, puzzle making involves cutting numerous small parts. Cutting these small parts without the aid of a clamp and fence to hold the stock would be very dangerous. Of course, woodworking is an inherently dangerous pursuit. It is therefore foolish to add to that danger.

**The author's** puzzle-making jigs take up an entire wall in his shop.

While precision and repeatability are reasons 1b and 1c why we usually use jigs, safety is reason 1a to use them for puzzle making.

This section covers the jigs that are used throughout the book. They are used in many, if not most, of the puzzles featured. There are a few other jigs that are used only once and for only one puzzle. They are covered in the instructions for that puzzle.

## Materials for Jigs

The material for your jigs will most often come from what is available in your shop. I usually make mine from a combination of a good-quality Baltic birch plywood and scrap hardwoods. Since jig stability is very important for

**Baltic birch plywood** is a good choice for making your jigs.

consistency, I try to make my jigs as strong and stable as possible. I even know a few puzzle makers who have gone to the expense of having elaborate jigs made from machined aluminum, with ball-bearing guides for the miter slot and all the bells and whistles.

### HARDWARE

When using many of these jigs, you will also need the assistance of a clamp or two. I use a variety of hold-down and push clamps. They

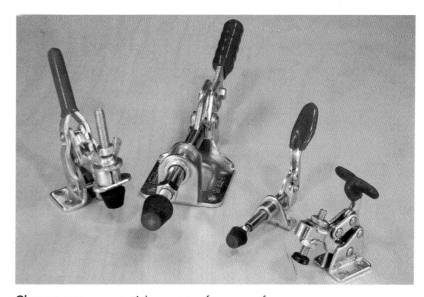

**Clamps are** an essential accessory for many of the jigs used in puzzle making.

## A FEW RULES FOR ALL JIGS

- Examine all your jigs thoroughly for any loose or missing parts before you use them.

- Double-check and adjust any clamps that may have become loose or were changed for a different-size stock.

- Be sure your sawblade is at 90° to the surface of your jig.

- Check frequently for any buildup of sawdust or small pieces of wood, which may alter the positioning of your stock in the jig. Check all surfaces of the jig and also the miter slots.

- Always check your first cut with the dial calipers before proceeding with any further cuts.

- Above all, do not become complacent because you think the jig is doing all the important work. If you get careless, accidents can still occur.

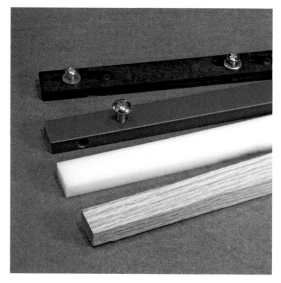

**Materials available** for miter-slot guides include (from top to bottom) plastic, metal, UHMW plastic, and hardwood.

come in a few different sizes and can be adjusted to fit most of your needs. You will see these clamps used on a jig when common sense prevents you from placing your fingers in harm's way.

One other item that's important for any jig used on a tablesaw is the miter-slot hardware. You can, of course, cut hardwood to use for your miter-slot guide bars, but if you're planning on making a lot of puzzles, I recommend investing in something a little more durable. There are several types of hardware available for this purpose. One of my favorites is ultra-high molecular weight (UHMW) plastic. It comes in $\frac{3}{8}$-in.-thick sheets, which is perfect for my tablesaw. The plastic cuts easily and can be run through a drum sander, so I can fine-tune the fit for my miter slot, and UHMW slides nicely without sticking. You can purchase enough UHMW plastic for several jigs for just a few dollars. Whatever material you use for the guides, always remember to give the bottom and miter-slot guides of your jigs a good coating of wax to keep them sliding freely.

# Ripping Jig

In my shop, I have a tablesaw that is 30+ years old and still has the original fence. This fence was never very accurate and, consequently, I seldom used it. Instead, I have resorted to a ripping jig for my tablesaw. Although this jig probably makes this process a bit longer for me, it makes up for it with accuracy I could not otherwise obtain. Whether you need a ripping jig like mine is up to you (for most woodworkers, it's probably not necessary). If you feel you need one, follow the plan and make the necessary adjustments for your particular saw.

**To use the ripping jig,** place the stock flush against the stock and hold it in place with the three clamps.

## RIPPING JIG

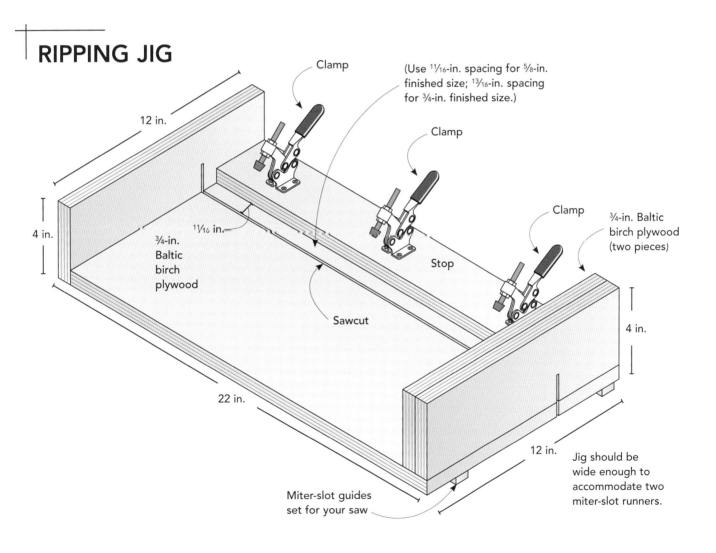

Clamp

(Use $^{11}/_{16}$-in. spacing for $^5/_8$-in. finished size; $^{13}/_{16}$-in. spacing for $^3/_4$-in. finished size.)

Clamp

12 in.

4 in.

Clamp

$^3/_4$-in. Baltic birch plywood (two pieces)

$^3/_4$-in. Baltic birch plywood

$^{11}/_{16}$ in.

Stop

4 in.

Sawcut

22 in.

12 in.

Miter-slot guides set for your saw

Jig should be wide enough to accommodate two miter-slot runners.

**The crosscut sled** is the workhorse of the author's puzzle-making shop.

**This is the operator's** side of the crosscut sled, showing the blade safety cover. Ventilation holes in the Plexiglas® top allow a dust collector to draw the chips in as the sled passes over the throat plate of the saw.

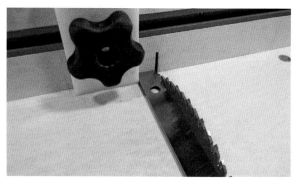

**The adjustable stop block,** made from UHMW plastic, stands up to the repeated bumping of stock when making the many cuts necessary for a batch of puzzles. It also sits flush to the base of the crosscut sled to prevent it from twisting when being tightened, and the firmness of the material makes for more accurate setup when using the set-up bars (as shown here).

# CROSSCUT SLED

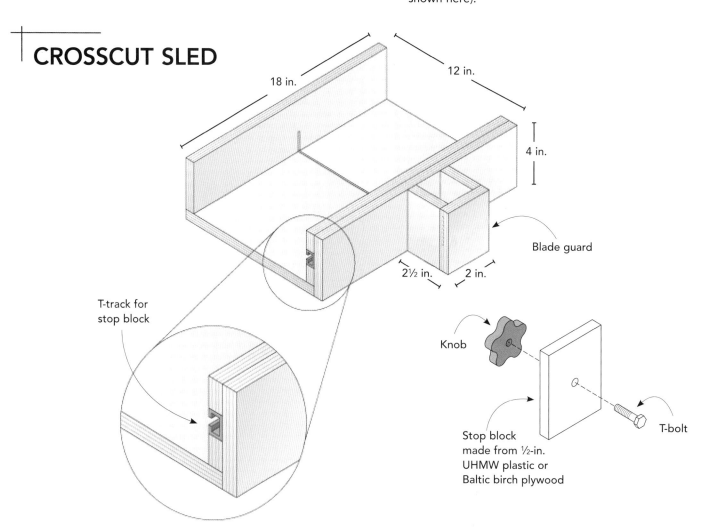

18 in.

12 in.

4 in.

Blade guard

2½ in.     2 in.

T-track for stop block

Knob

T-bolt

Stop block made from ½-in. UHMW plastic or Baltic birch plywood

# Crosscut Sled

The crosscut sled is one of the staples in most workshops with a tablesaw. It is by far my most frequently used jig. One of the great things about a crosscut sled for puzzles is the size. It doesn't have to be a 4-ft. x 3-ft. behemoth that requires several people to lift. But it does need to be adjustable and accurate. One of its primary features is an easily adjustable stop block made from UHMW plastic that will wear well, standing up to the abuse from sliding stock against it repeatedly.

# Corner-Gluing Jigs

The corner-gluing jig is another valuable jig for puzzle making. It consists of three pieces of plywood glued together at right angles to one another. The only dimension to consider is that the jig should fit most puzzles, which can run up to 3 in. to 4 in. wide. If you make your jig roughly 5 in. to 6 in. on all three sides, most puzzles should fit well.

I also use a large flat-gluing jig when I need a good 90° corner to reference pieces against but require more flat surface area than height. I suppose you could make a large flat-gluing jig with higher sides, but I am often working on several different types of puzzles at the same time, so the two serve me well. Once again, the dimensions are not critical, but accuracy of all the 90° corners (X, Y, and Z axis) is important.

**The corner-gluing jig** is one of the easiest jigs to make, requiring just three small pieces of plywood.

# CORNER-GLUING JIG

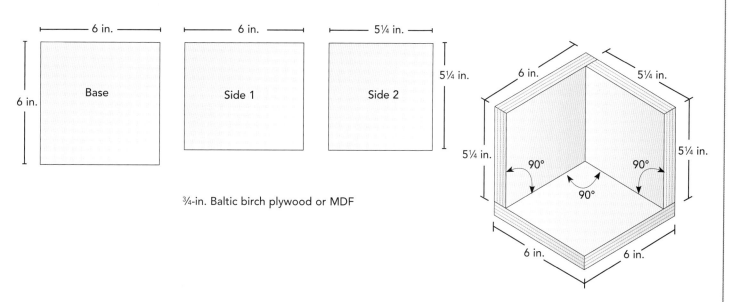

| 6 in. | 6 in. | 5¼ in. |
|---|---|---|
| Base | Side 1 | Side 2 |

6 in. (Base height)
5¼ in. (Side 2 height)

¾-in. Baltic birch plywood or MDF

6 in. · 5¼ in. · 5¼ in. · 5¼ in. · 90° · 90° · 90° · 6 in. · 6 in.

**Careful alignment** of the sides is crucial when gluing up the large flat-gluing jig.

**Keep the gluing jig** waxed to prevent excess glue from adhering to it.

# LARGE FLAT-GLUING JIG

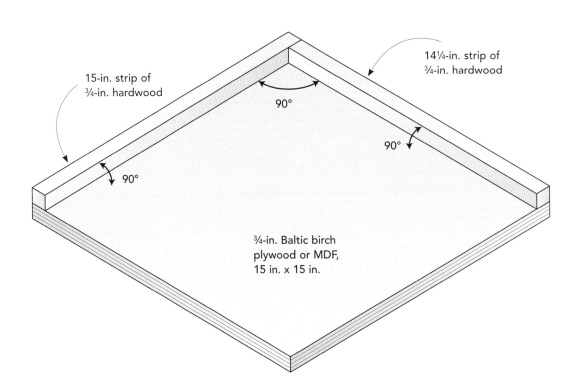

15-in. strip of
¾-in. hardwood

14¼-in. strip of
¾-in. hardwood

90°

90°

90°

¾-in. Baltic birch
plywood or MDF,
15 in. x 15 in.

# Edge-Beveling Jigs

Edge beveling is important because it allows puzzle pieces to slide against one another more easily. And bevels are often used to improve the overall look of a puzzle. Two types of edge-beveling jigs are used throughout this book. You could possibly get by without either one, if you prefer not to sand your corners. But when making puzzles with multiple cubes, you will quickly see the benefit of such a jig.

To make the long edge-beveling jig, rip two pieces of plywood or hardwood at a 45° angle (always double-check that your cuts are accurate). Glue the ends of the two mitered strips to a piece of hardwood at each end, with a gap of approximately ³⁄₁₆ in. between the strips. Make sure this gap is consistent throughout its length. Now, place your guide on top of a piece of 150- to 180-grit sandpaper. Depending on the width of the bevel you desire, you can shim your jig with tape or veneer to raise it above the sandpaper until the desired width is achieved. By sliding your stock back and forth in the guide, you should obtain an even bevel.

**The long edge-beveling jig is used for manual beveling of puzzle pieces.**

**Cut two mitered strips for the long edge-beveling jig. Accurate 45° cuts will ensure smooth operation of the jig.**

## LONG EDGE-BEVELING JIG

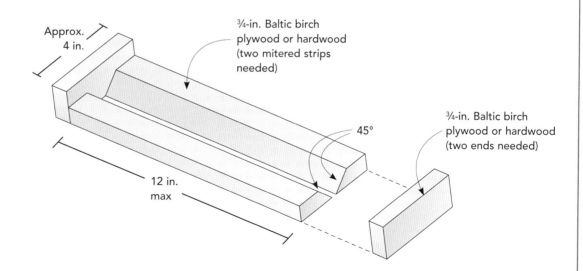

Approx. 4 in.

¾-in. Baltic birch plywood or hardwood (two mitered strips needed)

¾-in. Baltic birch plywood or hardwood (two ends needed)

45°

12 in. max

**The short edge-beveling jig,** used with a disk sander, is ideal for beveling corners that measure 1½ in. or less. This version of the jig has guides on two edges so you can make two different bevels. Simply turn it around to use the other edge for a slightly wider bevel. It is sometimes helpful to hold your jig in place with a spring clamp. The bottom view (right) shows the two different miter-slot guides.

# SHORT EDGE-BEVELING JIG

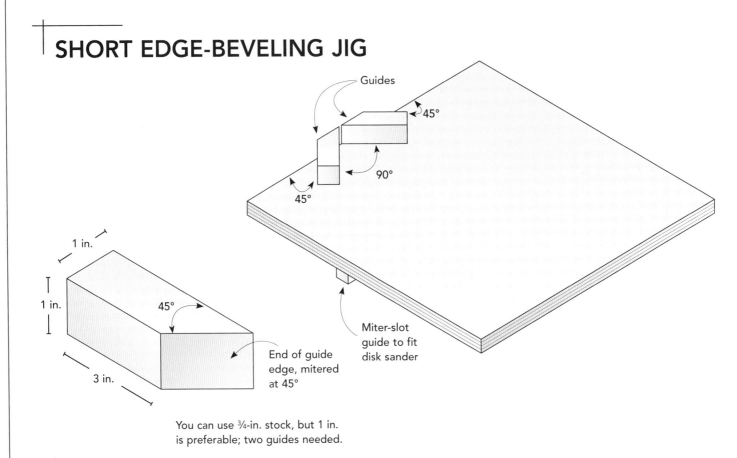

Guides

45°

90°

45°

Miter-slot guide to fit disk sander

1 in.

1 in.

45°

3 in.

End of guide edge, mitered at 45°

You can use ¾-in. stock, but 1 in. is preferable; two guides needed.

The other, short edge-beveling jig is intended for use on a disk sander. (If you don't own a disk sander, you'll need to make the long edge-beveling jig.) I tried making an adjustable version of this jig to perform both edge-beveling operations but abandoned them in favor of a separate jig for each size bevel. The jigs are relatively easy to make and require little material, so making several is not much work. And you will have better consistency than with an adjustable jig.

## CORNER-CUTTING JIG

The corner-cutting jig is similar to the edge-beveling jig but is made for the tablesaw, not the disk sander. One big difference in design is the push clamp used to hold the stock in place (and to keep your fingers out of harm's way). This jig essentially performs the same function as the short edge-beveling jig, but it does so much more aggressively. Instead of simply giving a slight bevel to the edge of a cube, this jig is capable of taking off much more material from the cube, creating another facet on the cube.

When using the jig, you will be able to cut off only half of the 12 edges of a cube before adjusting the clamp to remove material from the other 6 edges. This is because the jig removes so much material that the clamp will no longer meet up with the cube when the clamp is set to cut the opposing side of a previously made cut. Although this adds time to the operation, your fingers are well worth the effort!

**On the short edge-beveling jig** veneer can be glued to the face of each guide to reduce the width of the bevel. Different brands of sanding disks can also vary in thickness, which will affect the width of the bevel. This same method of veneering can be used on the corner-cutting jig (see p. 28) to change the width of a cut.

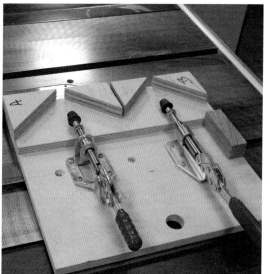

**The author made** his corner-cutting jig with two different bevel guides so he could make two different-width cuts. This one jig can handle cubes from 5/8 in. to 1 1/8 in.

**The clamp on the** corner-cutting jig holds the cube to keep your fingers away from the blade. Once you've made the first six cuts, you will need to adjust the clamp since it will no longer reach the side of the shortened cube.

# CORNER-CUTTING JIG

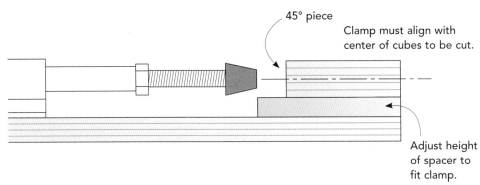

45° piece

Clamp must align with center of cubes to be cut.

Adjust height of spacer to fit clamp.

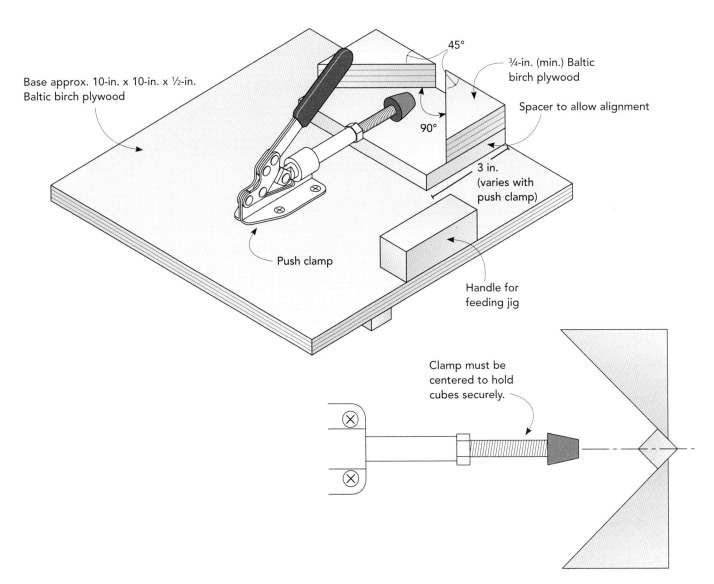

Base approx. 10-in. x 10-in. x ½-in. Baltic birch plywood

45°

90°

¾-in. (min.) Baltic birch plywood

Spacer to allow alignment

3 in. (varies with push clamp)

Push clamp

Handle for feeding jig

Clamp must be centered to hold cubes securely.

# Diagonal-Cutting Jig

The diagonal-cutting jig is probably the most difficult jig to make accurately, but it will reward you with impressive-looking puzzle pieces. It is used for the Triumph and Vega puzzles in this book, and there are myriad other puzzles that can be made with this jig. Essentially, the diagonal-cutting jig takes your stock, stands it on one of its corners at a 45° angle, and holds it at a 45° angle to the blade as you cut it. You may need to make several adjustments to get the cut just right, but if you can make accurate 45° cuts on your saw, you should not have much trouble.

## MAKING THE JIG

1 Cut the plywood base, which should be wide enough to accommodate a guide in each miter slot. I made my base 15 in. x 22 in. Add fences (approximately 4 in. high) to each end of the base and install the miter-slot guides on the underside of the base.

2 Cut two beveled pieces at 45° for the cradle. Trim 1/16 in. to 1/8 in. off the mitered edge of each piece.

The diagonal-cutting jig. The clamps are very close to the blade and should be checked for the proper clearance before making your first cut. You should never use a clamp to hold a piece in such a way that it binds against the blade once cut. Such pieces should be left to fall away on their own and removed once your blade has stopped.

Make a slight relief cut along the edge of the beveled piece to allow room for sawdust and small pieces of wood. Failure to do this will require you to stop and clean your jig more frequently.

# DIAGONAL-CUTTING JIG

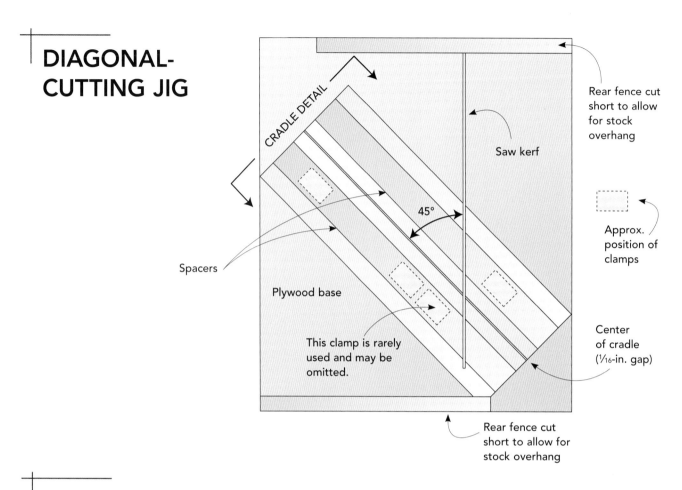

CRADLE DETAIL

Rear fence cut short to allow for stock overhang

Saw kerf

Approx. position of clamps

45°

Spacers

Plywood base

This clamp is rarely used and may be omitted.

Center of cradle (1/16-in. gap)

Rear fence cut short to allow for stock overhang

## CRADLE DETAIL

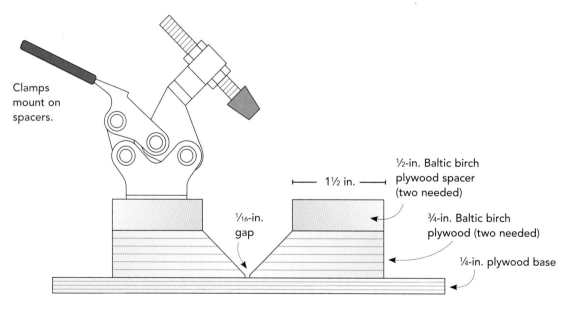

Clamps mount on spacers.

1½ in.

1/16-in. gap

½-in. Baltic birch plywood spacer (two needed)

¾-in. Baltic birch plywood (two needed)

¼-in. plywood base

3 Glue the beveled pieces to a base of ¼-in. plywood (you can also use ⅛-in. hardboard or Masonite). Make sure to maintain consistent spacing between the mitered pieces.

4 Glue spacers to the tops of the beveled pieces for the clamps. The size of the clamps you use will determine how thick you need to make the spacers. Remember, you are placing stock in this jig at a 45° angle, so 1-in.-thick stock turned 45° becomes a little more than 1⅜ in. thick. This completes the cradle assembly.

5 Once the base assembly has dried, place it on your tablesaw and make a cut the length of the jig. Use this cut to determine 45° angles for attaching the cradle assembly to the base. You can use a combination square or a drafting triangle placed up against the blade on the jig base to strike a line that you use to align the cradle. Attach the cradle assembly to the base with several screws, making sure that the screws do not protrude through the base of the jig.

6 Make your first cut through the beveled pieces before screwing any clamps in place.

7 Attach the clamps to the jig, referring to the top drawing on the facing page for positioning. Be certain they do not contact the blade; check for this with the blade raised high.

8 Place a piece of stock in the jig and clamp it in place. Make a test cut and check the stock for an accurate 45° cut. If necessary, loosen some of the screws (leave one in as a pivot point), make the necessary adjustment, and retighten the screws before making another test cut. Repeat this process until you have a perfect miter.

**Glue the beveled** pieces to the plywood base, maintaining consistent spacing between the pieces. Glue the spacers to the tops of the beveled pieces.

**Attach the cradle** to the base, and make your first cut through the cradle before screwing any clamps in place.

**Clamp the stock** in the cradle, and make a test cut to check the angle.

# THE PUZZLES

# BEFORE YOU BEGIN

This book contains plans and instructions for many types of puzzles, including square-stock puzzles, polyhedral puzzles, and a few miscellaneous puzzles. Even though all the puzzles are different, there is a common thread running through many of the instructions. Familiarizing yourself with some of the more frequently used practices will make your puzzle-making experience a little bit easier and hasten your success. In addition, I recommend building the Five-Piece Solid Block puzzle first (see p. 36). Many of the steps repeated throughout the book are covered in more detail in that first puzzle.

**It's important to** begin every puzzle with straight, evenly dimensioned stock. These sticks are ready to be passed through the planer for final dimensioning.

**Check all your**
milled stock (especially store-bought
stock) for square.

## Stock Preparation

As you work your way through this book, you'll
notice that square sticks are the basic building
block of most puzzles. The majority of my puzzles are made from stock that has been milled to
⅝ in. x ⅝ in. x 20 in. You can use whatever
length you are comfortable with, but I find that
20 in. is most convenient for me.

Milling your stock to be straight and square
is an important first step in any woodworking
project, and puzzle making is no different.
Unless you plan to work with premilled stock
that you purchased from a home center, you will
need to flatten and square one edge on a jointer
and bring the stock close to final thickness on
your planer. I say close to final thickness because
accuracy is important. If you give yourself a bit
of extra stock in the thickness and rip it close to
final width, you can then run your stock back
through the planer, rotating it 90° on each pass
to achieve your final dimensions. If you have a
drum sander, you can also use that to bring your
stock to final dimension.

Remember to check the dimensions of your
stock frequently. You are trying to get as close to
your desired dimension as possible. I like to be
within 1 or 2 thousandths, a degree of accuracy
that makes every future step of the process
much easier. All of the jigs I build are designed
to hold this same stock, either in stick form or

**Accurate dimensions are critical** to success-
ful puzzle making, so keep your dial calipers
handy and use them frequently.

| UNIT AND PUZZLE SIZES | | |
|---|---|---|
| NUMBER OF UNITS<br>H X W X D | DIMENSIONS<br>OF SINGLE UNIT | FINISHED SIZE<br>OF PUZZLE CUBE |
| 3 x 3 x 3 | ¾ in. x ¾ in. x ¾ in. (0.75 in.) | 2¼ in. x 2¼ in. x 2¼ in. |
| 4 x 4 x 4 | ⅝ in. x ⅝ in. x ⅝ in. (0.625 in.) | 2½ in. x 2½ in. x 2½ in. |
| 5 x 5 x 5 | ⅝ in. x ⅝ in. x ⅝ in. (0.625 in.) | 3⅛ in. x 3⅛ in. x 3⅛ in. |
| 6 x 6 x 6 | 9⁄16 in. x 9⁄16 in. x 9⁄16 in. (0.5625 in.) | 3⅜ in. x 3⅜ in. x 3⅜ in. |
| 7 x 7 x 7 | ½ in. x ½ in. x ½ in. (0.5 in.) | 3½ in. x 3½ in. x 3½ in. |
| 8 x 8 x 8 | 7⁄16 in. x 7⁄16 in. x 7⁄16 in. (0.4375 in.) | 3½ in. x 3½ in. x 3½ in. |

a smaller cut piece. As a result, straight stock will fit your jigs better and give you much better results. If your stock is not milled correctly to begin with, the jigs will do little to help you make a good puzzle. These jigs are tools, used to turn your sticks into beautiful wooden art. Or as world-renowned puzzle designer/maker Stewart T. Coffin calls them, "Ap-art, art that comes apart."

## Sizing Your Puzzles

For each puzzle, I've provided dimensions in the instructions, though, for most puzzles, these dimensions are not mandatory. The puzzles can be made smaller or larger at your discretion. The only thing that is critical is the consistency throughout a puzzle plan. Many puzzles are made up of units or cubes. Even a puzzle with a long stick is made up of a multiple of its width. For example, a puzzle that contains a stick that is 5 units long would be 5 times as long as it is wide (¾ in. x ¾ in. x 3¾ in.). The table above shows some general guidelines for puzzle size in units. These dimensions are only guidelines. It

should be noted that, as a beginner, the larger you can work, the better. Small pieces have tighter tolerances and, consequently, less room for error. However, for aesthetic reasons, the puzzle should not be too large and should fit nicely in your hand.

## Gluing and Finishing

All the glue-ups in this book are made with standard wood glue. Although I frequently use Titebond® III for exotic wood, any wood glue, cyanoacrylate (CA) glue, or even epoxy may be used in puzzle building. For the most part, the inexpensive wood glue that you probably already have in your shop is sufficient.

My preferred finish for my puzzles is spray lacquer because it dries fast. Puzzles often have many small pieces, and finishing could otherwise become quite tedious and time-consuming. After the lacquer dries, I apply a coating of paste wax or finishing wax and buff to a soft shine. This gives the puzzle a nice, soft feel and allows it to go together smoothly. After the wax has been buffed out, you can play with your puzzle.

# FIVE-PIECE SOLID BLOCK

*by Stewart T. Coffin*

I often sold my puzzles at craft shows, and this five-piece block puzzle was always the hands-down favorite, especially among younger visitors to my table. It is a classic Stewart T. Coffin design and possesses most of the characteristics that I feel make a great puzzle. With only five pieces making up the small cube, it is not overly complicated. All the pieces are different and irregularly shaped, and it only has one solution. While multiple solutions are sometimes desirable (such as the Distorted Cube on p. 108), in this case, the end result is only one shape, a cube, making the one solution more difficult to find. (The solution is presented on p. 140.)

## Cutting the Stock

1 As with any puzzle, the first step is to square your stock (see p. 34), surfacing all four sides as you would for any woodworking project. You'll need thirty ¾-in. cubes (27 for the puzzle and 3 extras just to be safe), so a piece of ¾-in. x ¾-in. (0.75-in.) stock about 30 in. long will be fine.

2 To make the first cut, set the stop on the crosscut sled using a machinist's set-up bar that measures ¾ in. (0.75 in.). Make sure that the set-up block just touches the very tip of the

carbide tooth of your blade and not the side of the blade. If you do not have set-up bars, you can use a piece of the ¾-in. stock you will be cutting for this puzzle.

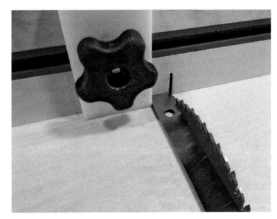

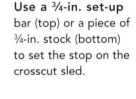
Use a ¾-in. set-up bar (top) or a piece of ¾-in. stock (bottom) to set the stop on the crosscut sled.

**The set-up bar** should touch the tip of the blade tooth, not the side of the blade.

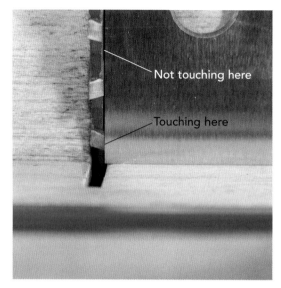

Not touching here

Touching here

**Add one or two** pieces of blue painter's tape to the side of the stop to shorten a piece you are cutting. To lengthen the piece, move the stop farther from the blade.

**Hold the stock** securely in place with a pencil eraser, applying steady downward pressure only. Any sideways pressure could cause kickback.

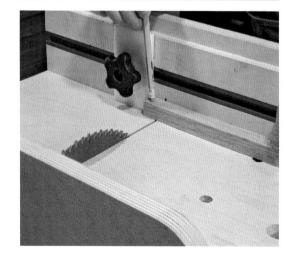

3 Check the dimensions of the first piece cut, and make any necessary adjustments to the crosscut-sled stop. For microadjustments, you can apply a piece of blue painter's tape to the side of the sled's stop block. The tape is about 0.0025 in. thick, and it can be used to shorten the length of cut by the thickness of the tape. If you find you need to add more than one or two pieces of tape, it is better to move the stop a bit. I try to get the desired dimension to within 1 or 2 thousandths (checking with dial calipers).

4 After getting the jig accurately set, cut 30 cubes (or a multiple of 30, if you are making more than one puzzle). Keep in mind that you are working with very small pieces here, so take great care with the cuts. You can use hold-down clamps to secure the stock, but in the interest of production, I favor holding the part securely with a pencil eraser.

## Beveling the Cubes

1 After all the pieces are cut, bevel all 12 edges of each cube on a disk sander with the short

edge-beveling jig (see p. 26). This not only helps the pieces fit together a little more smoothly, but it also adds a nice look to the puzzle. I use 120-grit paper to sand the bevels because it doesn't clog as quickly as a finer grit—and you will be giving the puzzle a final sanding later.

2 Check to make sure that the bevels are a consistent width along their length. A bevel that is wider at one end means that the jig is not perpendicular to the face of the sanding disk.

**Bevel all 12 edges** of the cube, applying consistent pressure so that the bevel is a consistent width from the top to the bottom of each edge (below).

## Gluing Up the Cubes

With the edges of all the cubes beveled, you are ready to start gluing. Every puzzle begins with a plan, or layout map. Some plans are quite complex, but for this cube puzzle with smaller cubes as the building blocks, the only real plan needed is the layout of how the pieces are glued together.

Remember that this is a five-piece puzzle. I glue the puzzle together in place and build the cube as I go along, using the layout map shown below. Pay careful attention to the plan, especially how the pieces are glued together between layers. If you fail to glue two pieces together as needed, it's not a big problem. You can always go

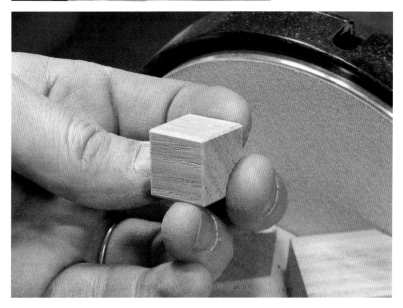

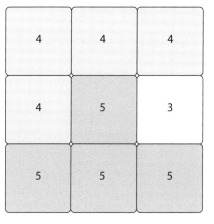

| 1 | 2 | 2 |
|---|---|---|
| 1 | 1 | 2 |
| 1 | 2 | 2 |

Bottom layer

| 1 | 3 | 4 |
|---|---|---|
| 4 | 3 | 3 |
| 5 | 2 | 3 |

Middle layer

| 4 | 4 | 4 |
|---|---|---|
| 4 | 5 | 3 |
| 5 | 5 | 5 |

Top layer

back and do so after the fact. However, inadvertently gluing together pieces that should not be glued will result in a puzzle that doesn't work or doesn't come apart at all. Take some time to familiarize yourself with using this map as similar diagrams are used for other puzzles in this book.

## GUIDELINES FOR GLUING

When gluing small puzzle pieces, you need to apply an even coating of glue but take care not to use too much. Tolerances are very tight and any squeeze-out should be removed immediately with a toothpick.

Pay close attention to grain appearance and direction when gluing up the puzzle. Just as with any woodworking project, grain can have an impact on the appearance of your puzzle. A consistent look is desirable if you are only using one species of wood. I also like to orient the pieces with the grain running in the same direction. This helps with any wood movement problems because all the pieces will move in the same direction.

A thin, even coating of glue that does not go all the way to the edges of the cube works best.

1 To begin, assemble the bottom layer and glue the pieces together following the map. The first layer will, therefore, consist of four #1s glued together and five #2s glued together. Starting with the second layer, you must now add, in the back corner, a #1 piece by gluing it to the piece below it. This completes the #1 piece.

2 Continuing on the second layer, add a #3 piece to the right of the #1 piece and a #4 next to that to complete the back row. The #3 and #4 pieces you just added are not yet glued to anything. Now add a #4 piece (again, without

**Use the corner-gluing jig** (see p. 23) for gluing up the cubes.

**The first layer.** Here, the #1 pieces are highlighted in red and the #2 pieces in blue.

glue) in front of the previously placed #1. Next, add another #3 and glue it to the #3 behind it. Add another #3 to complete the second row and glue it to the #3 to its left.

**3** Add a #5 piece to begin the third row, which will be glued later. Add a #2 piece in the middle of row three and glue it to the #2 piece below it. The last piece on the second layer is a #3 piece that is glued to the #3 piece behind it.

**4** Continue adding the pieces to the third layer, watching for pieces that get glued to pieces below as well as to adjacent pieces.

**5** When you have finished the top layer and glued all the necessary parts together, you need to make sure that everything is tight and square. Check the alignment and adhesion of everything by pressing on the sides and top of the puzzle. Some puzzle makers like to clamp the puzzle in the corner-gluing jig, using a piece of plywood about the same size as the puzzle on

**Continue adding** pieces to the second layer. Here, the #3 pieces are yellow and the #4 piece is green.

each of the three exposed sides. I find that applying pressure by hand for a few moments is sufficient. The glue bonds relatively quickly.

## Stewart T. Coffin

I have always considered Stewart to be *the* reason I started making wooden puzzles. From the moment I first saw his design of the Four-Piece Serially Interlocking Cube, I was hooked. While many of his designs are fiendishly complex, I am drawn to those that are simpler yet elegantly designed. A few of my favorites are featured in this book.

Like many designers of puzzles, Stewart got into puzzles at an early age when his Tinkertoy® set captured his attention and spurred an interest in geometric constructions. He has been producing wooden puzzles since the early 1970s, often enlisting the help of his wife and three daughters in those early years. His book, *Geometric Puzzle Design*, features more than 300 of his designs.

Although now retired, Stewart remains active in the puzzle community and lives in Massachusetts.

**The five finished** pieces should look like this.

## Taking the Puzzle Apart

1 Now comes the fun part. Your puzzle should come apart smoothly, as long as you managed to avoid squeeze-out and cut your pieces accurately.

2 You may now give the puzzle a light hand sanding using 180- or 220-grit sandpaper.

**The sanding mop** makes quick work of relieving the edges on irregularly shaped pieces.

I prefer to take it over to my drill press, where I have installed a sanding mop. I give each piece a quick pass over the sanding mop of 220 grit, lightly relieving the edges and smoothing the sides.

3 Apply a finish of spray lacquer to the five puzzle pieces.

4 After the lacquer dries, apply a coating of paste wax or finishing wax and buff to a soft shine.

Always show the puzzle to a potential victim in its solved state. Then quickly take it apart as you hand it to him and let him struggle to put it back into the original cube shape! With a non-interlocking puzzle, the challenge is the assembly.

**TIP**

**If any side of a cube** has blemished or unattractive grain, use that side as the gluing surface to hide the imperfections.

# LITTLE KENNY

## *by Ken Irvine*

L ittle Kenny is a newly designed puzzle by Ken Irvine. When I approached Ken about using one of his designs in my book, he was happy to contribute. As a matter of fact, Little Kenny is the only puzzle that was designed just for this book. With this new design, we are going to take what you learned with the Five-Piece Solid Block and take it a few steps further. This puzzle resembles the Five-Piece Solid Block in that it is made up of cubes glued together to form a larger cube (or rectangle). But Little Kenny is an interlocking cube (see the sidebar on p. 45), and it requires some sliding of pieces to solve it. (The solution is presented on p. 141.)

I love puzzles with sliding pieces, which introduce an entirely new level of complexity to the puzzle. One piece must be moved out of the way so that another can move. This type of movement is not always obvious, and the better made your puzzle, the more difficult the movement is to detect. Your goal is to create snug-fitting parts that have just enough friction to keep them from falling out but are still easily removed with just a touch of pressure. With a puzzle like this, accurately cutting and beveling the cube edges will aid in the playability.

**Begin by cutting** the ⅝-in. cubes and then bevel the edges.

**Following the map,** glue up the 16 cubes in the bottom layer: seven cubes for the #1 piece, four cubes in the center for the #2 piece, and five cubes for the #3 piece.

## WHAT YOU NEED

- Approx. 36 in. of ⅝-in. stock (or two 18-in. lengths of contrasting woods to make the checkerboard pattern)
- Crosscut sled
- Set-up bars or blocks
- Dial calipers
- Wood glue
- Edge-beveling jig
- Corner-gluing jig

# Preparing the Cubes

1 Using ⅝-in. square stock, begin by cutting 48 cubes (24 of each wood if you're using the contrasting colors). You will need only 45 cubes for the puzzle, but the others are used as spacers in the construction process. Cut your cubes as described in the Five-Piece Solid Block directions (see p. 37).

2 Bevel the edges of these cubes in the edge-beveling jig at the disk sander. A narrow bevel is sufficient for this puzzle. Although there are sliding pieces, they do not add any difficulty to the gluing process.

# Gluing Up the Cubes

1 Following your map and using the corner-gluing jig, glue up the bottom layer of the puzzle. If you are using contrasting woods, there is nothing different about the glue-up other than that you must pay attention to which type of wood to glue in place. The pieces themselves do not change. As with the Five-Piece Solid Block puzzle, I have identified the parts by both a color and a number. The bottom layer contains only three of the four parts to this puzzle.

2 Position the second layer so the blocks that make up the fourth piece are along the back and side. Add the #2 piece in the corner. You will need to use the spacers (colored red in the photo) to complete the second layer. With your spacers in place, continue gluing up the rest of the second layer. Once the glue has set up (five to 10 minutes), you can remove the spacers with a piece of tape.

3 Before adding the top layer, glue together two pairs of cubes. These cubes will be used on the top layer (for the #1 and #2 pieces), and they will span an area where there is nothing beneath them. Gluing them in pairs now will allow you to glue them in place without the

## INTERLOCKING VS. NONINTERLOCKING PUZZLES

You will often see puzzles referred to as interlocking or noninterlocking. This distinction is not always obvious when looking at a puzzle. Interlocking puzzles (such as Little Kenny) usually require removal of a "locking" piece. Without the removal of the locking piece, no other pieces can be removed.

**Add two spacers** (highlighted in red) to the second layer. The voids that will be left by the spacers are where the pieces need to slide to when disassembling the puzzle.

**Complete the** second layer, then use a piece of blue painter's tape to remove the two spacers.

| 1 | 1 | 3 | 3 |
|---|---|---|---|
| 1 | 2 | 2 | 3 |
| 1 | 2 | 2 | 3 |
| 1 | 1 | 1 | 3 |

Bottom layer

| 4 | 4 | 4 | 4 |
|---|---|---|---|
| 4 | 2 |   | 4 |
| 4 |   | 1 | 3 |
| 4 | 4 | 1 | 3 |

Middle layer

| 3 | 3 | 2 | 4 |
|---|---|---|---|
| 3 | 2 | 2 | 4 |
| 3 | 1 | 1 | 4 |
| 3 | 3 | 3 | 3 |

Top layer

**Glue together** two pairs of cubes (#1 and #2 pieces) that will span the void left by the spacers.

+

**TIP**

**Remember to remove** the two spacers before adding the pieces in the top layer. The voids left by the spacers allow the pieces to slide, and the puzzle will not be usable if the spacers are left in place.

support from below. If you are using contrasting woods, you will need one of each wood as shown.

4 When the second layer has dried and the glue is set on the cube pairs, begin gluing the blocks in the top layer. Start in the back corner and glue the #3 pieces, adding the remaining pieces and using the glued-up pairs for pieces #1 and #2. These will be placed over the empty spaces in the middle layer. Even though there is nothing under one half of the pairs, they should stay in place as they are held there by the surrounding pieces.

## Ken Irvine

Ken, who is an engineer with master's degrees in electrical engineering and computer science, has been collecting puzzles since the early 1970s. His wife, Helene, kept saying that he should design his own puzzle. He eventually broke down and created his first puzzle design, called, at his wife's suggestion, the "Nagging Wife."

Since he started meeting with puzzle collectors from around the world, Ken's perception of what makes a good puzzle has changed. "Most metagrobologists (people who study puzzles) enjoy puzzles that are fun, not trivial, have an 'aha' factor, and are not impossible to solve without a computer," says Ken. "I try to use that as a guideline when developing puzzles."

Most of Ken's hobbies are centered around puzzles and have followed a natural progression over the years: solving, collecting, designing, and crafting. I was very pleased that "Little Kenny," design #47 for Ken and named after his first grandchild, was developed specifically for this book.

5 Finish off the top layer by adding the remaining cubes in pieces #3 and #4.

6 Periodically check the top layer pairs by applying light pressure to the various pieces. Because this puzzle is interlocking and has pieces that slide, it is important to allow the glue to dry completely. Once dry, you can take apart your new puzzle. The individual pieces are shown in the photo below.

To finish, apply a coat of spray lacquer and then paste wax or finishing wax. Because the puzzle has sliding pieces, it's important to finish with the wax.

**The completed** puzzle.

This is what the four pieces of the disassembled puzzle should look like.

# THREE-PIECE BLOCK

## by Stewart T. Coffin

The Three-Piece Block is another Stewart T. Coffin design. As with all of Stewart's work, it is simplistic in its design but fiendishly difficult to solve. Most people really struggle with this one. Consisting of just three parts and made from only 10 pieces of wood, it is one of the quickest puzzles to make. However, it requires the con-

struction of a rather tricky gluing jig shown in the photo below (dark brown wood).

We will cover the building of the jig first, but you can cut all your material at once because the jig is made from the same ³⁄₄-in. cubes as the puzzle. You will need 10 cubes for the jig and 10 cubes for the puzzle. As ever, I recommend cutting a few extra cubes. Also, this puzzle goes

## WHAT YOU NEED

- ¾-in. x ¾-in. x 24-in. stock (you can also make the jig from a secondary or contrasting wood as shown here, in which case you would need a 12-in. length of each wood)
- Crosscut sled
- Dial calipers
- Wood glue
- Corner-gluing jig
- Edge-beveling jig (for the puzzle pieces, not the jig pieces)
- Pyramid glue-up jig (made for this puzzle)

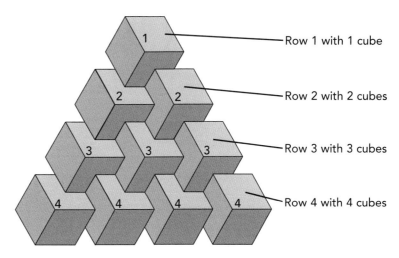

Row 1 with 1 cube

Row 2 with 2 cubes

Row 3 with 3 cubes

Row 4 with 4 cubes

Gluing jig viewed from above

together rather quickly, so you may want to cut enough to make a few for friends. It takes much longer to make the jig than it does the puzzle.

In addition to the 10 cubes that make up the jig, you'll need several extras to use as spacers when making the jig. You could certainly use a few of the cubes from the puzzle, but you run the risk of getting some glue on areas where it may show, so I recommend cutting the extras. I'm using pieces cut from a contrasting wood as spacers for clarity; you may want to do this as well. You will also need a few half-cube spacers. The plan calls for ¾-in. cubes, so the half-cube spacers should be cut to ¾ in. x ¾ in. x ⅜ in. Accuracy when cutting these jig pieces and spacers is every bit as important as when cutting the actual puzzle pieces.

**TIP**

**For some jigs,** I like to bevel or soften the edges, but for this jig I prefer not to because it gives you more flat surface and stability, which is needed here.

# Making the Jig

1 Begin by cutting about fifteen ¾-in. cubes and five ⅜-in. half-cubes. I used walnut, a contrasting, darker wood for clarity, but of course you can use all the same species for your jig and puzzle. I also cut some extra red oak pieces for the spacers (again, for clarity).

Before you begin gluing the jig, take a look at the drawing, which shows how the cubes are arranged when glued. You need to take care here because it is very easy to build the jig as a mirror image. If you do, the jig is still usable, but you

**To build the pyramid** gluing jig, begin by placing one half-spacer in the corner-gluing jig and set a full cube on top of it.

**The first cube** with the two half-spacers in place.

**Apply glue** to only one-quarter of each face when making the jig; be sure not to go beyond that.

**Add the second** cube, gluing it to the first by its quarter-face.

**You will be adding** either full or half-spacers with each successive piece to raise them up and shift them over. Substitute a full spacer for two half-spacers when necessary.

will have to mentally flip all the gluing of the puzzle pieces and the solving will also be slightly different. I can speak from experience on this!

2 To glue the first two jig pieces together, you'll need two of the half-spacers. Place one half-spacer flat into the corner of the three-sided gluing jig as shown in the photo on p. 49, and place a full cube on top of it. The spacers do not get glued.

3 Stand another half-spacer on edge and to the left side of the pieces in the jig. This will offset the jig piece enough to allow for only a quarter-face to touch the adjacent cube. Now apply glue to just the upper corner of the next jig piece. Place the glued piece up against the full cube, with the spacer to the left. Apply light pressure to be sure of a good bond. Your first two cubes are now glued as shown in the center photo at left. You can handle the jig pieces after just a few minutes, which is long enough for the wood glue to set up, but handle them carefully so they don't come apart.

4 Reposition the spacers, adding another row of steps behind the ones in place in the jig so you can glue the third cube in the first row (see the top left photo on the facing page). After this piece has dried, add a fourth set of spacers behind the existing ones. This should be one half-level higher than the existing spacers. You are essentially creating a pyramid with the spacers. This lets you align each cube to be one half-face above and one half-face to the right of the one behind it.

You should now have a set of four cubes as shown in the center photo on the facing page. This completes the first, and longest, row needed for the jig.

**5** Repeat the process to make a smaller row of three cubes and then another row of only two cubes, leaving one more for the top row of the jig. These are the four pieces that will be glued together to make the jig.

**6** Take the row of four cubes and nest the row of three cubes against it as shown in the bottom photo at right, using one of the half-blocks as a spacer to align the two rows. The half-spacer block should line up with the edge of the block in the next row. If you made your cuts accurately and your spacers are accurate, these pieces should fit together tightly. Now mark the areas where the two rows touch with a pencil and apply glue to these areas; realign the pieces to glue them together. It's important to make the pencil marks the first time you make this jig. As you will see, the many faces of the different cubes can be very confusing.

**7** Add the row of two cubes in the same way, and finish with the last cube glued in the last corner. Carefully compare your assembly with the photo on p. 52 as you progress through the glue-up of the jig. Each cube is attached by a quarter-face to each adjacent cube.

**8** Once it dries thoroughly, your jig is ready. Apply a good coat of paste wax to help keep squeeze-out from adhering your puzzle to the jig. I also recommend softening the edge of the jig with fine-grit sandpaper.

**TIP**

**Keep the wood grain** running in the same direction as you glue up the jig pieces. I have oriented the grain so that it runs vertically in this jig.

**You can now** begin to see the stair-step process as cubes are added. Each cube (or cubes) gets raised and spacers added to align the front cube with the next quarter-face.

**Continue to stack** additional spacers in the gluing jig, and add the fourth cube.

**The finished row of** four cubes for the jig.

**Use one of the** half-spacers to align the edges of the first two rows of cubes.

**The pyramid glue-up jig** is assembled, ready for use to make the puzzle pieces.

# Building the Puzzle

Follow the gluing map below to build the puzzle. Take the time to fit each piece into place without gluing, and verify correct placement by comparing it to the map. Also, take extra care to note where the pieces will be glued together. Some pieces will be glued only on their quarter-face, while others will be glued by a half-face. Still others will be glued by two different faces to adjoining cubes. To help minimize the effects of any wood movement, orient the grain of the wood in the same direction for all the pieces.

1 Before you begin the glue-up, lightly bevel the edges of the 10 cubes that you cut for the puzzle. This makes assembling the puzzle a bit easier and compensates for any slight misalignment.

2 To begin the bottom layer, first glue the three #1 pieces by their quarter-faces. Add the two #2 pieces and glue them together by their quarter-faces also. Add the single cube for the #3 piece for gluing later. That completes the cubes for the bottom layer.

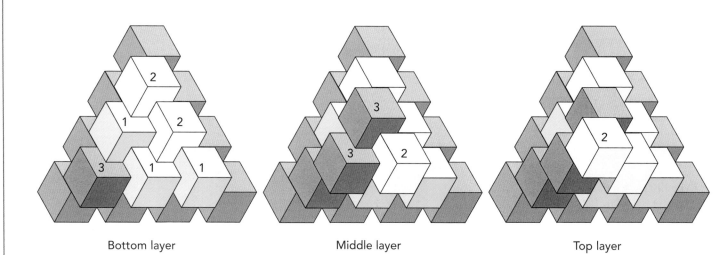

Bottom layer          Middle layer          Top layer

## MAKE AN EXTRA PUZZLE

The Three-Piece Block, more than any other puzzle in the book, is where mistakes are made when gluing—not surprising given the confusion of the angled cubes with different gluing surfaces. It's a good idea to assemble a spare copy of the puzzle in the jig first and use a marker to number all the cubes with their relevant piece numbers (1, 2, and 3). Then reassemble the puzzle using just enough glue for a temporary hold. Using these pieces as a guide, you can better familiarize yourself with how the puzzle goes together. Ten cubes is a small sacrifice to avoid frustration

thing into alignment. After the glue has dried, you are ready to disassemble the three pieces and to begin the difficult task of trying to solve the puzzle! (The solution is presented on p. 143.)

**The bottom layer** of the puzzle in place in the jig.

**The top layer.**

3 Allow the bottom layer to dry for a few minutes, then start the middle layer by adding the next two #3 pieces. Note that the first of these is glued to the existing piece by its half-face and the second by its quarter-face. Glue the middle-row #2 piece to the existing #2 pieces below it by its half-face.

4 The final piece of the puzzle is another #2 piece glued by its half-face to the #2 piece in the middle row. Apply light pressure on the three faces of the puzzle to help bring every-

**The three pieces of the puzzle should look like this when finished.**

# CONVOLUTION

*by Stewart T. Coffin*

I discovered the Convolution puzzle early in my puzzle-making career. I was fascinated by the symmetrical pattern and the interlocking sequence, so I made a few copies and they sold well at the craft shows I attended. The Convolution is also well suited to using contrasting woods to achieve an interesting pattern (see "Taking Your Puzzles to the Next Level" on p. 134).

The instructions given here are for making the Convolution puzzle, but another similar puzzle named the Involution, also by Stewart T. Coffin, shares all the characteristics of the Convolution except for the solution. Both are made from the same components, both have the same symmetrical pattern on all six sides, and both have the same placement of several of the individual pieces. They simply get glued together differently, resulting in a different solution. Coffin may have viewed the Involution as an improvement on the Convolution design, but I'm not sure that I would agree. I think they are both superb designs, and, like the Five-Piece Solid Block (p. 36), they are relatively easy to make. Do a little research and see if you can discover how to make the Involution, too.

## PARTS LIST

| SIZE | QUANTITY | DIMENSIONS |
|---|---|---|
| 1-unit piece | 16 | 5/8 in. x 5/8 in. x 5/8 in. |
| 2-unit piece | 24 | 5/8 in. x 5/8 in. x 1¼ in. |

## WHAT YOU NEED

- Approx. 50 in. of 5/8-in. stock
- Crosscut sled
- Set-up bars or blocks
- Dial calipers
- Wood glue
- Corner-gluing jig
- Edge-beveling jig

## Preparing the Pieces

1 Begin by setting up your crosscut sled to cut sixteen 5/8-in. x 5/8-in. x 5/8-in. single-unit pieces and then twenty-four 5/8-in. x 5/8-in. x 1¼-in. two-unit pieces. Remember to use the set-up bars or a piece of stock between the blade and the stop block to get the proper spacing (see p. 38). Make a test cut on a piece of scrap, and verify that the cut is exactly 5/8 in., or 1¼ in. for the two-unit piece, before cutting the remaining pieces.

2 Bevel the corners of each piece. This puzzle requires the rotation of a piece to remove it (see the solution on p. 144), and the beveling helps quite a bit with the rotation and the many sliding moves. Use the edge-beveling jig at the disk sander for both the one-unit and two-unit pieces. (I don't recommend beveling anything longer than a two-unit piece with this jig because it can be difficult to maintain a consistent bevel width.)

**Stand the two-unit** pieces on end to bevel the long side in your edge-beveling jig at the disk sander.

Bottom layer

Second layer

Third layer

Top layer

**Beginning on the** bottom layer, glue up a cube and a double cube for piece #3 in the corner-gluing jig.

**It's important to** apply the glue carefully, both to achieve a good bond and to avoid squeeze-out.

**Glue up the first** two double cubes for piece #4 (purple) and set them over piece #3.

# Gluing Up the Puzzle Pieces

The glue-up of this puzzle is the trickiest part of the construction. I provide detailed instructions for the bottom two layers here; use the same process to assemble the top two layers. For clarity, the photos show the pieces with the color that corresponds to the gluing map on p. 55. It's essential that you familiarize yourself with the gluing map—not just for the Convolution but also for most puzzle plans in the book. I still use this map to make my Convolutions, even though I have made hundreds.

1 Gather all your parts, both single- and double-unit pieces, the three-sided corner-gluing jig, and some wood glue. Begin the puzzle by placing a one-unit piece (now referred to as a "cube") in the back corner of the jig and glue a two-unit piece (now referred to as a double cube) to it as shown in the top photo at left. This is the beginning of piece #3 (yellow). Note that the numbers of the pieces relate to their order when assembling the puzzle, not the order in which you will be gluing them together. Also keep in mind that, on the double-cube pieces, you will usually only be applying glue to a little less than half of a face. Make sure you do not overdo it to avoid squeeze-out.

---
TIP

**Throughout the book,** I refer to puzzle pieces by the number of units they are. In other words, a cube ⅝ in. x ⅝ in. x ⅝ in. is a one-unit piece; a piece measuring ⅝ in. x ⅝ in. x 1¼ in. is a two-unit piece; a piece ⅝ in. x ⅝ in. x 1⅞ in. is a three-unit piece, and so on.

2 Add two double-cube pieces as shown in the bottom photo on the facing page. Both of these are part of piece #4 (purple) and get glued together as they rest on piece #3.

3 Continue to add pieces, working out from the corner of the jig by adding another double-cube piece to #4 (purple) and gluing it to the adjacent piece. Then add a cube to the front left corner to be part of piece #2 (blue) and a vertical double cube to the other end to be part of #6 (gray). Add a cube (yellow) next to the #6 gray cube to be glued up to the other pieces of part #3 later; this will be the back right corner cube. Add one more double cube (red) horizontally in front of the right corner cube (yellow).

4 For the next step, you'll be gluing four cubes together into two pairs, as shown in the center photo at right. You might ask why you couldn't just use a double cube. You could, but the objective here is to preserve the symmetry of the puzzle, even when it cannot be seen. I appreciate that I am being a bit of a purist here, so feel free to use a double cube instead if you'd prefer. Just remember to adjust the parts list accordingly. The first of these two pairs of cubes is a #3 (yellow) piece, and half of this assembly will be glued to the existing piece #3 below it.

5 Add a double cube on top of the #2 piece (blue) in the front left corner and glue them together. Place a double cube in position and glue it to the #3 cube in the back right corner and the double-cube pair to the left of it. Place a double cube (#1, red) vertically in front to the right of the #2 pieces, as shown in the bottom photo at right. Now place a double-cube piece (red) in the bottom row and glue it to both the double cube in the back and the vertical double cube you just placed on its left. Slide the second double-cube pair, a #2 (blue) pair, in behind the #1 pieces (red) and glue it to the #2 (blue) cube to its left.

**Following the** gluing map, continue to add pieces, working out from the corner of the gluing jig.

**Glue a pair of** yellow cubes together, then glue them to the existing #3 piece below.

**The second glued-** up pair (blue) slides in behind and on top of two glued #1 pieces (red).

**Add #3 (yellow)** and #2 (blue) pieces to complete the first two layers.

**The completed puzzle.**

The seven individual pieces should look like this when the puzzle is disassembled.

6 Place a vertical, double cube in front of the right corner pieces (yellow) and glue the top half to the piece behind it. Place a cube in the near corner (a #2, blue piece) and add a double cube on top (blue), gluing it to both the corner cube you just added below and the double-cube pair behind it. You are now done with the first two layers.

7 Now continue placing the pieces onto the next two layers following the map carefully. When completed, your puzzle should look like the one in the center photo at left—without the colorization, of course.

8 When the pieces are completely dry, disassemble the puzzle; the pieces should look like those in the bottom photo at left. You may need to refer to the solution on p. 144 to take your puzzle apart the first time.

While this gluing process may seem a bit confusing at first, once you understand the map and can visualize the pieces above and below your current piece as well as the ones that are adjacent, I think you will find it gets pretty easy. (Although I must admit that my occasional lack of attention has led to a few very attractive pieces of firewood!)

## Finishing the Pieces

The Convolution is a perfect example of why I prefer to spray my puzzles with lacquer. As you can see, the pieces are all irregularly shaped, which makes applying a finish by brush or wiping on a fairly time-consuming process. Factor in the rapid drying time of the lacquer, and you have much more time to make additional puzzles.

# THE ELEVATOR

*by Jos Bergmans*

The Elevator takes some of the characteristics of Little Kenny (see p. 43) and then adds a few twists . . . literally! This is what is known as a rotational cube, and designer Jos Bergmans is the master of this kind of puzzle. I have often wondered how a designer could come up with so many variations using only the small 4 x 4 x 4 or in this case 4 x 4 x 5 space. Rotational cubes do require special attention both to cutting accuracy and to the gluing process. Sometimes the tolerances for these rotations can be very tight, and if a piece is misaligned or a bit too long, it may not work. One of the most important things about rotational puzzles is remembering to bevel the edges.

A rotational cube will test your skills as a puzzle solver when you try to disassemble the built puzzle. Some puzzle craftsmen prefer to build the pieces individually and assemble everything afterward, but I like to glue up this type of puzzle "in situ" or fully assembled. I think you get a better result and a more workable puzzle in the end.

## Planning the Puzzle

Now is a good time to address the piece breakdown of puzzles like this. Early on in the puzzle-building process, I take the map for the puzzle I

## WHAT YOU NEED

- Approx. 60 in. of ⅝-in. stock
- Crosscut sled
- Set-up bars or blocks
- Dial calipers
- Wood glue
- Short edge-beveling jig
- Long edge-beveling jig
- Corner-gluing jig

| PARTS LIST | | |
|---|---|---|
| SIZE | QUANTITY | DIMENSIONS |
| 5-unit piece | 4 | ⅝ in. x ⅝ in. x 3⅛ in. |
| 4-unit piece | 4 | ⅝ in. x ⅝ in. x 2½ in. |
| 3-unit piece | 6 | ⅝ in. x ⅝ in. x 1⅞ in. |
| 2-unit piece | 7 | ⅝ in. x ⅝ in. x 1¼ in. |
| 1-unit piece | 10 | ⅝ in. x ⅝ in. x ⅝ in. |

**Bottom layer**

| 1 Vert. | | 4 Vert. | | 1 Vert. |
| 1 | 2 | 4 4 | 4 | |
| 3 | | | | 3 |
| | | 2 | 2 Vert. | |

*Bottom layer*

| 1 Vert. | 2 Vert. | 4 Vert. | 4 Vert. | 1 Vert. |
| 1 | | | | |
| 3 | | | | |
| 3 | 2 | | 2 Vert. | 3 |

*Second layer*

| 1 Vert. | 2 Vert. | 4 Vert. | 4 Vert. | 5 Vert. |
| 5 | | | | |
| 6 | | | | |
| 6 | | 2 Vert. | 6 | |

*Third layer*

| | | | 4 Vert. | 5 Vert. |
| 6 | 2 | 4 | 5 | |
| | | | 4 | 6 |
| | | 2 | 2 Vert. | 2 |

*Top layer*

**TIP**

**Use the color-coded** photos as a guide for when to pause and assemble the next group of pieces. Take the time to familiarize yourself with how they will go together.

am making and I do a piece analysis. I try to determine several things: I want to use as many large pieces as possible, I want to try to get as many long-grain to long-grain joints as possible, and I want to consider any possible patterns on the exterior of the puzzle. This last factor rarely comes into play, but it can be important to the overall appeal of a puzzle if you are able to establish any kind of pattern.

All of these factors play out in the piece list. Up to this point in the book, we have used only single and double cubes for the puzzles. But the Elevator has several rotations and sliding parts. The fewer joints there are, the easier the puzzle will be to play with. Considering all these factors —and which ones are more important to you as a puzzle builder—may lead you to change your piece list. This puzzle is 5 x 4 x 4 units with a two-unit hole in the front. Therefore, there are 78 units in all. How you arrive at those 78 units is up to you. After you have made the puzzle shown here, see if you can come up with a piece breakdown that better suits you.

You'll also note that this puzzle incorporates more sticks that are placed vertically. You must

**Gather all the parts** for the puzzle pieces, the three-sided corner-gluing jig, and some wood glue.

**Glue the two #1 pieces (red) in the corner, then place the first #3 (blue) and #2 (yellow) pieces.**

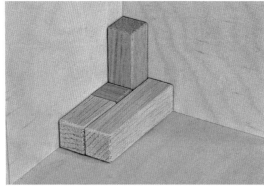

**Continue working out from the corner, adding pieces to the base and back wall.**

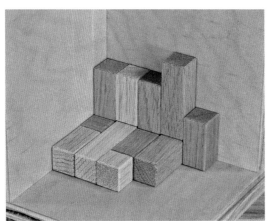

be thinking in three dimensions when assembling this one, so pay attention. I have provided the usual map for you to follow but have also included color-coded photos. Compare the two as you go along with the glue-up. This will help you understand the relationship of the vertical pieces in the map.

## Construction

1 After cutting all the parts, bevel the edges. This is a step I recommend you take with all rotational cubes. Although beveling is not absolutely essential, it's helpful when pieces must rotate in small spaces, especially for a beginner puzzle builder. Use the long-edge beveling jig for the longer pieces. Follow with a light sanding to remove any fuzz or rough edges. Do not remove any surface wood; just clean up your pieces.

2 Begin by placing a vertical 3-unit piece (#1, red) in the corner and glue a single-unit piece (#1) in front of it. Without using any glue,

## Jos Bergmans

Jos got into designing puzzles when he purchased a few wooden puzzles at a Christmas market while visiting family in the Netherlands. Jos says, "I liked them, but I thought I could do a better job of it." Well, I think he proved himself right! Jos now has about 80 designs, and he seems to have an affinity for rotational cubes. "I love the simplicity of a 4 x 4 x 4 design. A good puzzle should not take more than 30 minutes to solve but should not be easy either." Pirouette, his favorite puzzle, offers all of these features, plus an interesting rotation. The Elevator puzzle, shown here, is another of his rotational cube designs with a few different rotations in the solution.

Jos is a software engineer at Google and lives in Southern California. When not designing puzzles, he likes woodworking, electronic design, and gardening.

lay a 2-unit piece (#3, blue) in front of them and add a 4-unit piece (#2, yellow) alongside of these.

3 Stand a 2-unit piece (#2) against the 3-unit piece (#1) in the corner, and glue it to the 4-unit piece (#2) below. Stand a 3-unit piece (#4, purple) alongside the #2 and glue a 2-unit piece (#4) to its base. Glue a single unit (#2) to the #2 alongside it. Then lay a 3-unit piece (#4) alongside the existing #4 and stand another 3-unit piece (#4) on top of it and glue them together. Finally, place a vertical 2-unit piece (#1) alongside the #4 pieces, again without gluing. This completes most of the bottom layer, but because of the structure of this puzzle, we will continue with other layers before completing the bottom layer.

4 Continue to follow the gluing map and use the photos at right to complete each stage. Notice the use of a spacer in the center of the puzzle in the final image (dark brown). This walnut block can easily be slid out after the puzzle has dried. You can also use blue painter's tape to remove it.

## Finishing the Puzzle

Once the pieces are completely dry, disassemble the Elevator. As you remove pieces, make note of any areas where parts stick and lightly sand them until they slide smoothly with just a bit of friction to keep them from falling out. All that's left now is to apply your choice of finish and some wax. (The solution is on p. 146.)

**Most of the second** layer has been added at this point and some of the third and fourth.

**The third layer is** almost complete, except for the area that will contain the spacer and an adjacent block.

**With the fourth** layer almost complete, have a spacer piece ready for the final steps.

**Glue the single** cube (yellow) to the double cube in front, and place the spacer on top of it with no glue. Finish filling in the last few pieces around the spacer.

# SATURNO #1

## by Yavuz Demirhan

T he Saturno #1, by designer Yavuz Demirhan, is easy to build and appears to incorporate a "board" into the puzzle. Now you could simply cut a large piece of wood to the proper dimensions and, with the help of a drill press, a set of chisels, or a hollow chisel mortiser, start cutting the square hole into the board. But the beautiful thing about most puzzles like this is that they can also be glued up using the same square stock that you have been using all along.

By cutting the proper-length pieces and gluing them together according to the plan, you can get precisely positioned holes, or "notches," in the board, which accept the pieces that make up the rest of the puzzle.

## Making the Puzzle

For both clarity for the builder and appeal to the puzzle solver, we will make this puzzle from walnut and red oak. The board, or "frame," is

| PARTS LIST | | | |
|---|---|---|---|
| SIZE | QUANTITY FROM WALNUT (FOR THE FRAME) | QUANTITY FROM RED OAK (FOR THE PIECES) | DIMENSIONS |
| 5-unit piece | 3 | | ⅝ in. x ⅝ in. x 3⅛ in. |
| 3-unit piece | | 4 | ⅝ in. x ⅝ in. x 1⅞ in. |
| 2-unit piece | 1 | 4 | ⅝ in. x ⅝ in. x 1¼ in. |
| 1-unit-piece | 3 | 1 | ⅝ in. x ⅝ in. x ⅝ in. |

## WHAT YOU NEED

- Approx. 16 in. of ⅝-in. stock of two different species of wood (or 30 in. of one species)
- Crosscut sled
- Set-up bars or blocks
- Dial calipers
- Edge-beveling jig
- Wood glue
- Large flat-gluing jig

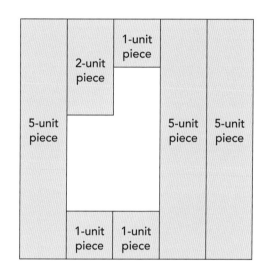

made of walnut and the three pieces from the red oak.

1 Cut all the pieces you will need.

2 Before beginning the glue-up, I recommend that you bevel the edges of the red oak pieces. These pieces need to slide against one another, and the edge beveling helps with that. I don't recommend that you edge-bevel the pieces for the walnut frame because this would detract from the illusion that the frame is a solid piece of wood. If you choose your wood carefully and the grain is consistent, you can create a frame that appears solid to the casual observer—thereby increasing the appeal of the puzzle.

**Follow the Parts List** carefully to make sure you cut the correct number of pieces for each species of wood (walnut for the frame and red oak for the puzzle pieces).

TIP

**The Saturno #1** is a rather small puzzle that does not require a great deal of wood, which makes it an ideal candidate for upgrading with exotic wood species as discussed in "Taking Your Puzzles to the Next Level" on p. 134.

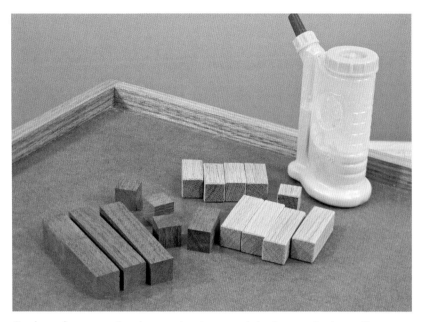

**Gather the parts** for the puzzle pieces and the frame, the large flat-gluing jig, and some wood glue.

**The frame awaits** the final piece.

**Allow the finished** assemblies to dry before making a test fit.

3 Glue up the frame based on the plan on p. 65, using the 5-unit pieces for the outer edges and filling in with the 2- and 1-unit pieces. It's a good idea to use a few of the red oak pieces as spacers in the opening of the frame to ensure you won't have too much sanding to do at the end.

4 Using the bottom photo at left as a guide, glue up the three edge-beveled red oak pieces while the frame is drying. The U-shaped piece comprises a 1-unit piece sandwiched between two 3-unit pieces. The two identical L-shaped pieces are each made with two 2-unit pieces glued perpendicular to a 3-unit piece, with a 1-unit gap between the 2-unit pieces. Again, use an extra piece to space out the pieces so that you have a better fit when assembling the puzzle.

5 Sand the frame flat by laying it on a piece of sandpaper and moving it in a circular motion. You can also use a random-orbit sander to flatten the frame. Try not to remove too much wood, and test-fit the pieces that go into the frame to be certain you have not made it too loose. The oak pieces should get a final hand sanding with 220-grit paper to remove any rough spots and relieve the edges, or give them a light pass with your sanding mop.

## Finishing the Pieces

Using the finish of your choice and a final waxing should make the pieces slide nicely without binding or falling out. Once more, the solution to this puzzle is not obvious, especially when assembling. Disassembly for this type of puzzle always seems easier to me. Eventually, you will try enough ways to remove the pieces that something will come out. The trick is whether you were paying attention to what you did! (The solution is presented on p. 149.)

# 8 PLAQUES = CUBE

*by Stéphane Chomine*

This puzzle combines a few of the styles that we have already seen. When you first look at the pieces, you may think it is a board burr, like the Bedevil puzzle featured on p. 74, since a few of the pieces intersect along a central axis.

However, upon closer inspection, you will see that this is actually a cube with some rather unique pieces. Designed by Stéphane Chomine, the 8 Plaques = Cube is a difficult puzzle to solve for the inexperienced. And if given to a rather serious puzzler in its unassembled state,

## WHAT YOU NEED

- Approx. 80 in. of ⅝-in. stock
- Crosscut sled
- Set-up bars or blocks
- Dial calipers
- Short edge-beveling jig
- Long edge-beveling jig
- Wood glue
- Large flat-gluing jig

### PARTS LIST

| SIZE | QUANTITY | DIMENSIONS |
|------|----------|------------|
| 5-unit piece | 4 | ⅝ in. x ⅝ in. x 3⅛ in. |
| 4-unit piece | 9 | ⅝ in. x ⅝ in. x 2½ in. |
| 3-unit piece | 4 | ⅝ in. x ⅝ in. x 1⅞ in. |
| 2-unit piece | 8 | ⅝ in. x ⅝ in. x 1¼ in. |
| 1-unit piece | 26 | ⅝ in. x ⅝ in. x ⅝ in. |

**Using the crosscut sled,** cut all the parts for the puzzle. Start with the 5-unit pieces and work your way down.

### TIP

**I recommend** using both beveling jigs for this puzzle because it has many of the smaller single-unit cubes. These take time to bevel but go much quicker on the disk sander. Make certain that your bevels are a consistent width if you do use the two different methods for beveling.

it can provide hours of frustration. (The solution is presented on p. 151.) One of the first of Stéphane's designs I built, it proved to be a winner, appealing to both young and old. A somewhat simple puzzle to make, it is also easily enhanced with contrasting or exotic woods.

## Preparing the Stock

1 Begin by cutting all the pieces based on the Parts List using the crosscut sled. Start with the larger pieces and work your way down, double-checking the first piece of each size that you cut for accuracy with your dial calipers. I also recommend that you cut one or two extras of each size piece. These can be used as spacers or if you make a mistake during construction.

2 At this point, you need to make a decision on the desired look of the puzzle. The 8 Plaques = Cube puzzle lends itself to beveling, but it is not necessary as long as you make the pieces carefully. I prefer not to bevel the pieces and just give the parts a light sanding to relieve the sharp edges after they are glued up. If you want to bevel the edges, do so now using the short edge-beveling jig on the disk sander and the long edge-beveling jig for the larger pieces.

# Making the Puzzle

1 To assemble the puzzle, you will use the large flat-gluing jig along with the puzzle map. My flat-gluing jig is approximately 16 in. square, which allows plenty of room to work on several pieces at a time. You are only using the corner of the jig to set the first piece or two. After that, you can move the piece over to one side and use a flat side to reference the remaining parts.

2 Gluing together each piece is a simple process because you're only working in one plane. As an example, for piece F, you will need two 4-unit pieces, two 2-unit pieces, and three 1-unit pieces. Working out from the corner of the flat-gluing jig, place a single-unit piece in the corner and add a 1-unit spacer before placing a 2-unit piece next to it. To these you will glue the 4-unit piece. Next, add a 3-unit piece as a spacer

**Use spacer blocks** (shown here in a darker, contrasting wood) to help with the alignment of the pieces. You can also use appropriately sized set-up bars to get the correct spacing.

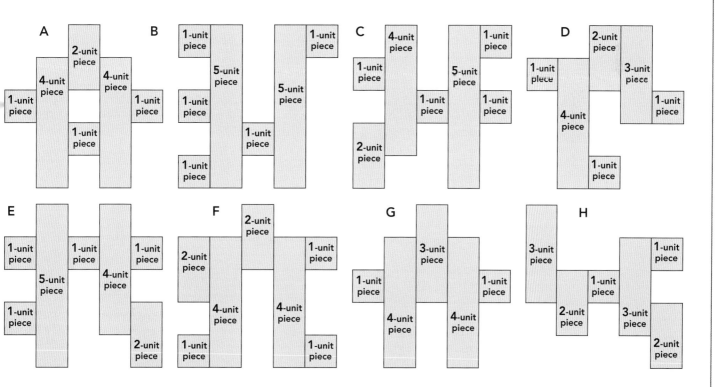

**The eight finished** pieces.

**If a hole is too** small for a piece to be inserted, glue a piece of sandpaper to a stick and remove enough wood for a better fit.

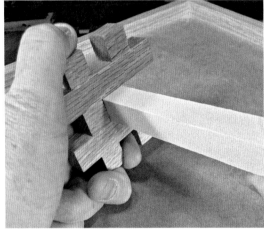

Be sure to get wax into (and out of) all the crevices of the puzzle before you do a final buffing out.

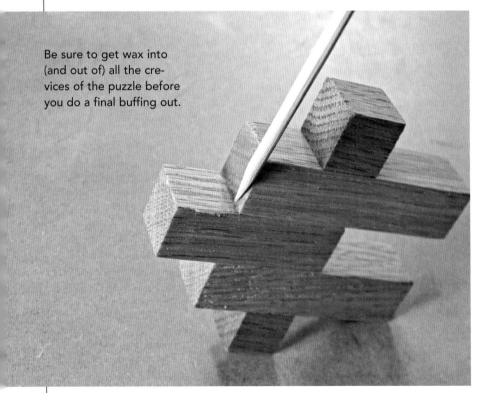

TIP

**Always glue up** the parts to get as much long grain-to-long grain gluing surface as possible. The parts for this puzzle could be glued up in several ways, but the layout shown gives good gluing surfaces and results in a strong puzzle.

and add the 2-unit piece so that half of it protrudes above the 4-unit piece you just glued into place. Keeping the spacers in place, you can now add another 4-unit piece, gluing it to half of the 2-unit piece. Lastly, add the two 1-unit pieces by placing the first, adding a 2-unit piece spacer, and gluing the second to the other end of the 4-unit piece.

3 When all eight parts have been assembled, they should look like the pieces in the top photo at left. Allow the pieces to dry, then do a test fit. Refer to the solution on p. 151 to see how to put the puzzle together. Everything should fit together without being forced. If it doesn't, place the problem piece or pieces on sandpaper and a flat surface. Move the piece in a circular motion, sanding the entire side of each piece. Test-fit the pieces together frequently while sanding so that you don't sand off too much material and make the puzzle loose.

4 If you have not beveled the edges, now would be the time to do a light sanding to soften the pieces.

5 Once everything fits together well, finish-sand the pieces and apply lacquer or shellac and a final coat of wax.

TIP

**Put some of the parts** together in ways that are not correct as well. You do this because any solver will do this, too. You want them to be able to try incorrect solutions, leading them down a path that will not work.

# KNOTTY 3

## *by Yavuz Demirhan*

K notty 3 is probably one of the easiest puzzles in this book both to build and to solve. However, all puzzles seem easy when you know the solution. If you were to hand the three pieces of this puzzle to anyone, show them a picture of the puzzle, and then ask them to solve it, most people would take longer than you might expect. Knotty 3 was designed by the Turkish designer Yavuz Demirhan, who also designed the Bedevil puzzle on p. 74. Knotty 3 is one of the few puzzles in this book where any minor construction problems can be solved during the finishing process. The shape of the pieces is basic, and, as long as you don't mind the puzzle being a little loose, any errors can be corrected with some sandpaper.

## WHAT YOU NEED

- Approx. 20 in. of ⅝-in. stock or 24 in. of ¾-in. stock
- Crosscut sled
- Set-up bars or blocks
- Dial calipers
- Wood glue
- Large flat-gluing jig

| PARTS LIST | | |
|---|---|---|
| SIZE | QUANTITY | DIMENSIONS |
| 4-unit piece | 3 | $5/8$ in. x $5/8$ in. x $1 7/8$ in. |
| 2-unit piece | 3 | $5/8$ in. x $5/8$ in. x $1 1/4$ in. |
| 1-unit piece | 6 | $5/8$ in. x $5/8$ in. x $5/8$ in. |

**With all 12 pieces cut,** you are ready to begin construction on the large flat-gluing jig.

The Knotty 3 also requires very little wood, making it a good candidate to create from exotic woods. Or try constructing each piece from a different wood to achieve a unique-looking puzzle.

## Making the Puzzle

All three pieces of the Knotty 3 are identical. They are also fairly simple in their structure. I made my puzzle from $5/8$-in. stock, but you can also use $3/4$ in. if you prefer. As always, accurate cutting is necessary, even though there is more margin for error with this puzzle.

1 Use the crosscut sled to cut the pieces. Remember to use set-up bars to get accurate cuts and double-check your dimensions with dial calipers.

2 Once you have all the pieces cut, gather your glue and the large flat-gluing jig for assembly. Place one of the 4-unit pieces into the corner of the jig and glue a single-unit piece to one end, as shown in the top photo on the facing page. Glue another 1-unit piece at the other end of the 4-unit piece. Rotate the piece in the jig to make sure the single-unit pieces are completely

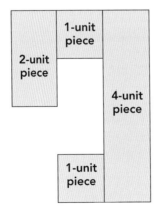
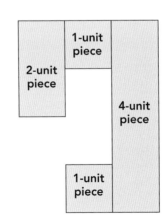
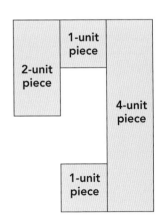

flush with each end of the larger piece. Check the fit by inserting one of the 2-unit pieces in between the single-unit pieces at the ends. It should fit snugly but come out with just a bit of friction. If it is too tight, allow one of the single-unit pieces to extend beyond the edge of the 4-unit piece. Set this aside and repeat the process two more times. You should now have three C-shaped pieces.

3 Now add the 2-unit piece to each C-shape, making it into a sort of J. If you had to adjust one of the single-unit pieces to extend beyond the end of the large piece, glue this 2-unit piece to the opposite end. This bottom foot gets inserted into the other pieces, and you don't want it to extend too far or it will not fit.

4 Allow all three pieces to dry thoroughly before removing any overhang on the ends of the pieces. Flat-sand the pieces by laying them on sandpaper and moving them in a circular motion; this will smooth out the pieces and help them slide together more easily. Relieve all the edges with your sanding mop or some 220-grit sandpaper. Apply a finish of your choice and then wax. The Knotty 3 is now ready to confound your friends and family. (The solution is presented on p. 153.)

(The solution is presented on p. 153.)

**TIP**

**Sometimes with** a board burr–type puzzle (see p. 74), the ends of the parts do not need to be that accurate. In this puzzle, if the pieces aren't perfect, you can flatten out the end without affecting the workings of the puzzle. You may create a gap that you didn't really want, but the puzzle itself will still work fine.

(see p. 74)

**For each of the** three pieces, begin by gluing a 1-unit piece to one end of a 4-unit piece.

**Glue another 1-unit** piece at the other end of the 4-unit piece, and use a 2-unit spacer to check the fit.

**If the outer edges** do not quite line up, you can correct it with a bit of sanding.

**Always keep a few** extra pieces around for use as spacers, which will minimize any extra sanding you need to do.

# BEDEVIL

## *by Yavuz Demirhan*

The Bedevil is an example of a type of puzzle known as a "board burr." A burr is a puzzle that consists of interlocking, notched sticks. In a board burr, these sticks are large flat pieces, more like a board. There are many types of board burr puzzles, and they vary in size and the number of boards that intersect. The Bedevil, by the Turkish designer Yavuz Demirhan (see the sidebar on p. 77), consists of five wide boards that intersect with each other along three axes. It is one of the less complicated board burrs to build

| PARTS LIST | | | |
|---|---|---|---|
| SIZE | RED OAK | WALNUT | DIMENSIONS |
| 7-unit piece | 4 | | ⅝ in. x ⅝ in. x 4⅜ in. |
| 5-unit piece | 3 | | ⅝ in. x ⅝ in. x 3⅛ in. |
| 4-unit piece | 2 | | ⅝ in. x ⅝ in. x 2½ in. |
| 2-unit piece | 10 | 1 | ⅝ in. x ⅝ in. x 1¼ in. |
| 1-unit piece | | 16 | ⅝ in. x ⅝ in. x ⅝ in. |

**A**

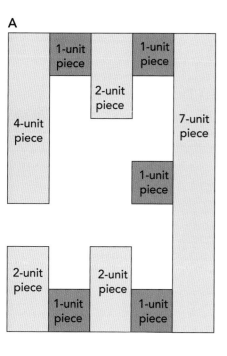

**B**

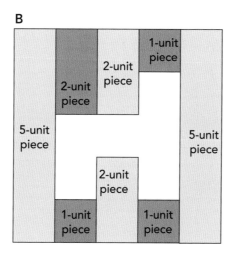

**C**

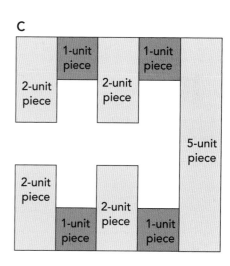

**D**

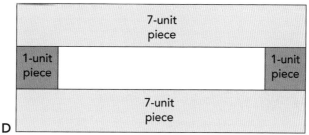

**E**

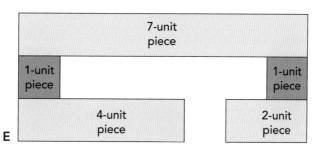

---

**TIP**

**Always start** by cutting the longest pieces first. That way, you can cut the smaller pieces from what is left over from cutting the longer pieces, resulting in less waste.

## WHAT YOU NEED

- Approx. 72 in. of ⅝-in. stock (18 in. and 54 in. of varying stock if using two contrasting woods)
- Crosscut sled
- Set-up bars or blocks
- Dial calipers
- Long edge-beveling jig
- Wood glue
- Large flat-gluing jig

**Using spacers** between the pieces being glued helps you achieve a better fit. Here, the darker walnut cubes are being glued to the 7-unit piece behind (this is the start of Part A). The spacers are the 2-unit oak pieces between the walnut cubes.

**The completed Part A.**

but is still rather difficult to solve. I really enjoy making and solving this style of puzzle; there are invariably moves that lead to a dead end or serve only to more deeply interlock the pieces.

Although it is not necessary to use contrasting woods for the puzzle, I chose to make mine from walnut and red oak. I did this for two reasons. First, I really like the way the contrasting woods look, and I think it adds to the interest of the finished puzzle. Second, it gives you a much better picture of how the individual pieces get glued together.

## Making the Puzzle

1 Cut all the pieces for the five parts of the puzzle following the Parts List on p. 75. Don't worry if you don't have a contrasting wood; it's fine to cut all the pieces from one species, such as red oak, if you prefer. When cutting all the parts, I recommend you cut at least one extra of each size. You can always use them for future puzzles if you don't need them for this one. A recap of the stock preparation process is given on p. 79.

You don't need to bevel the edges of the individual pieces at this point. You will bevel the edges after the parts are glued up (see p. 78).

2 Gather all the pieces and sort them by size to help simplify assembly. Use the gluing map on p. 75 to guide your glue-up on the large flat-gluing jig. As I assemble each part, I use some of the other pieces as spacers (see the top photo at left). You want the spacers to be snug but not so snug as to make removal difficult. Be careful about glue squeeze-out or you will need those extra pieces you cut.

3 For Part A, you will need one 7-unit piece, one 4-unit piece, three 2-unit pieces, and five single-unit pieces (see the bottom photo at left). The other four parts are glued up as shown in the photos on the facing page. Continue to

**For Part B,** you'll need two 5-unit pieces, three 2-unit pieces, and three 1-unit pieces.

**For Part C,** you'll need one 5-unit piece, four 2-unit pieces, and four 1-unit pieces.

**For Part D,** you'll need two 7-unit pieces and two 1-unit pieces.

**Finally, for Part E,** you'll need one 7-unit piece, one 4-unit piece, one 2-unit piece, and two 1-unit pieces.

# Yavuz Demirhan

Yavuz has long been one of my favorite puzzle designers, and I have probably produced more of his designs than those of any other designer. He caught my attention several years ago when I noticed how frequently he was posting new designs on Facebook. Yavuz continues to be one of the most prolific puzzle designers, having produced more than 400 designs since 2011. He says that a typical design can take anywhere from a few days to as little as a few hours to create.

Yavuz specializes in designing wooden puzzles. Trained as a carpenter, Yavuz incorporates his understanding of wood into his designs. Many puzzle designs are better suited to being manufactured in plastic or metal. But Yavuz's background as a woodworker has been instrumental in creating designs that work beautifully when made from wood.

Yavuz currently lives in Datca, Turkey, making puzzles from his home workshop. They can be found on his website: www.cubozone.com.

**Slide the finished** pieces into each other to double-check the fit and to see how much sanding may be necessary.

**Finish-sand the** pieces both flat (right) and on end (bottom right).

use spacers to ensure a snug fit. You'll do a light sanding at the end, which will alleviate any tightness and allow the parts to slide together smoothly yet securely.

## Final Fitting and Finishing

1 Once all your parts are dry, double-check that they fit. I like to try to slide them into each other (as shown in the top photo at left) to get a feel for how much sanding I will have to do.

2 If everything fits and slides nicely without binding, you can do just a light finish sanding. If the pieces bind, you may have to use a coarser (120-grit) sandpaper to remove a bit of wood from the flat sides or ends of the parts. Make sure to sand the ends to even them out. You should be able to do this by standing them on end and moving them in a circular motion on the sandpaper.

3 To give the puzzle a nice, professional look, I like to bevel the edges of the finished parts. The best way to do this is to use the long edge-beveling jig, as shown in the left photo on the facing page. Using a test piece first, place the jig over a piece of 180-grit sandpaper and slide the part back and forth along each outer edge to add the bevel. This will not only make the puzzle look better but also make it easier to insert one part into the other. Don't forget to add or remove tape to get the depth of the bevel you are looking for (see p. 25).

4 A coating of your choice of finish and an essential application of wax will keep your puzzle in good working order. (The solution is presented on p. 153.)

**Use the long edge-beveling jig** over a sheet of 180-grit sandpaper to bevel the edges of the finished parts.

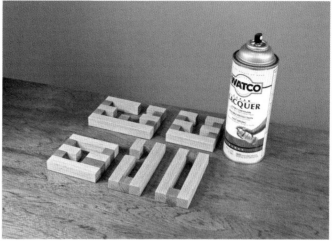

**The five finished** pieces await a coat of lacquer and wax.

## STOCK PREPARATION RECAP

I talked about stock preparation at the start of the Puzzles introduction (see p. 34), but it won't hurt to go over the key points again here. Taking a little extra care when preparing your stock will save hours of work later.

Always begin with straight, evenly dimensioned stock. Starting with ¾-in.-thick boards, I like to rip my stock close to final dimension, plane it down to within a few thousandths of final size, and then run it through my drum sander to "dial in" that final size. For the Bedevil puzzle, that dimension is ⅝ in. (or 0.625 in. if you have dial calipers that measure in thousandths). I usually cut my sticks to approximately 20 in. long. That's the length I find most convenient, but feel free to use whatever length you are comfortable with.

Once your stock is properly dimensioned, you need to accurately cut your sticks to the proper lengths. This is where the set-up blocks, mentioned in the Tools chapter (see p. 9), come into play. My set-up bars came with two bars of each size, in varying widths, from ½ in. to 1⅝ in. in ⅛-in. increments. With these bars I can achieve any length needed to make this puzzle. For example, to make the 5-unit pieces, I simply use two 1¼-in. bars and one ⅝-in. bar to get the 3⅛-in. length. For the 7-unit piece, two 1½-in. bars and one 1⅜-in. bar do the trick. Always make a test cut to verify that the piece is exactly the length you need to avoid a lot of unnecessary sanding.

# TWIN PENTOMINOES INTO A LIGHT BOX

*by Primitivo Familiar Ramos*

Here's a fun puzzle that requires you to fill a frame with what seems like an unending supply of pentominoes. A pentomino is a geometric shape that is formed by joining five same-sized cubes edge to edge. The pentominoes (or penta-cubes, as they have a three-dimensional shape) in this puzzle are all asymmetrical and consist of six mirrored pairs. These are the "Twins" referred to in the name. Precise cutting is required here to allow all of the possible "non-solutions" to be attempted by the solver. It wouldn't be as much fun any other way! As difficult as this puzzle is, there are thousands of ways to solve it. (See p. 156 for one solution.)

## WHAT YOU NEED

- Approx. 54 in. of ⅝-in. stock for the pentominoes
- Approx. 30 in. of ⅝-in. stock for the frame (contrasting color)
- A few small pieces of plywood approx. 2 in. x 3 in.
- Crosscut sled
- Set-up bars or blocks
- Dial calipers
- Short edge-beveling jig
- Wood glue
- Corner-gluing jig

| PARTS LIST | | | |
|---|---|---|---|
| SIZE | RED OAK | WALNUT | DIMENSIONS |
| 4-unit piece | | 4 | ⅝ in. x ⅝ in. x 2½ in.+ |
| 3-unit piece | | 8 | ⅝ in. x ⅝ in. x 1⅞ in.+ |
| 1-unit piece | 60 | | ⅝ in. x ⅝ in. x ⅝ in. |

## Building the Pents and Frame

The puzzle consists of two separate parts—the pentominoes and the frame, or light box—and we will use two different woods for contrast. You might want to consider building a second three-sided gluing jig for this puzzle so that you can work on both parts at the same time. Each pentomino is made by gluing up five of the 60 cubes into the various shapes. The result is six pairs of pentominoes. These 12 "pents," as I call them, will all fit into a frame that is 4 x 5 x 5 units.

To make the frame, you will be gluing some end grain on some of the pieces, which, as you know, is not the optimum situation. However, when making a cubed frame this way, I have found that each side is strengthened by being

**It's a good idea** to work with two corner-gluing jigs to speed up the process. That way, you can work on the pents and the frame at the same time.

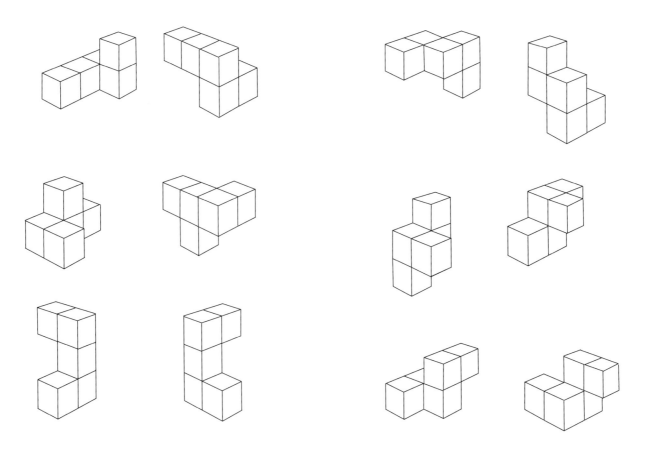

**Placing the cubes** in a zippered plastic bag and gently tossing them about will remove much of the fuzz that often appears on the back side of your cuts. The photo below shows the same cube after a minute or so in the bag. This trick also makes the edge-beveling process a bit easier.

**Use extra pieces** as spacers as necessary when gluing up the individual pents.

glued at both ends and one side, and each piece draws strength from all the other pieces in the frame. You can use more traditional joinery methods to improve the strength of the joints, but I have never found it necessary or worth the extra effort. In fact, I have stood on top of these boxes and with my 200 lb. have never been able to break one.

## Gluing Up the Pents

1 Let's begin with the pents. Cut at least 60 cubes using your crosscut sled on the tablesaw. As always, check for accuracy. I like to bevel the corners of these cubes. This is a time-consuming process, but you will find a rhythm . . . and it will go quickly.

2 Glue up the pents into the shapes shown in the drawing on the facing page. Use extra pieces as spacers as necessary. Notice that each of these parts has a mirrored twin. Use this to double-check that you have glued up your pieces properly. Set the pents aside to dry while you work on the frame.

## Building the Frame

1 Cut four pieces that are 4 units long and eight pieces that are 3 units long. Here, we are going to cheat and add just a few thou-

**The 12 pentominoes,** arranged in mirrored pairs.

**Cut the frame parts** a hair long, using a business card between the set-up bars and the stop block to add the extra length.

**Cut plywood** spacers to aid in the alignment of the frame.

**Begin building the first side** of the frame, using one of the plywood spacers to square up the frame.

sandths to each of these measurements, which will help you avoid hours of sanding to get the pentominoes to fit.

When setting the stop block on the crosscut sled, use the set-up bars (or stock) and add a business card or tape to the side of the stop block to add a few thousandths of an inch. After setting the stop block, remove the bars and business card and your stop block should be the desired length, plus a few thousandths.

2 Cut small pieces of ½-in. plywood into a rectangle that is 2 units by 3 units (plus the extra thousandths) using the same business card or tape to add a few thousandths to each dimension.

3 Now let's start building the frame. Using the corner-gluing jig, place one of the 4-unit pieces into the corner and glue one of the 3-unit pieces to it as shown in the left photo above.

## Primitivo Familiar Ramos

Primitivo is a mathematician and high school teacher who lives in Spain. When he was a child, his grandfather made a puzzle of wire, the Disentanglement Sweetheart, and since then the world of puzzles has always been his passion. He has been a fan of Martin Gardner (mathematician and author) and Yakov Perelman (noted science writer) since he was a child.

A puzzle collector for many years, Primitivo's main interest is in packing and burr puzzles. In addition to Twin Pentominoes into a Light Box and Murbiter's Cube (p. 96), other examples of his designs are Pack the Podium, the Stellated Burr, Alhaurin Challenges, Murbiter's Devilish Burr, and Menold's Trick Box (named after yours truly!).

This is where we incorporate the butt joint. Set one of the pieces of plywood in the frame, place the other pieces around it, and glue them into place, being careful not to get any glue on the plywood. You now have one side of the frame glued. Wait for the glue to set up a little, then gently remove the plywood. Check after removing it that the frame side is still square. Repeat this process for the other side of the frame.

**Keep adding frame** pieces and spacers for the other sides of the frame.

4 When the first frame side is dry, stand it up in the corner-gluing jig and glue another crosspiece into the corner. Insert another piece of plywood to keep everything straight, and add another crosspiece. Once dry, rotate the frame 90° and add another crosspiece. Also, add the plywood vertically to keep your spacing even. Rotate the frame once more and add the last crosspiece, adding the plywood as before.

5 You are now ready to attach the final side to the frame. Apply glue to all four posts, and place the last frame side into the jig. Set something heavy on top to hold the pieces together and recheck the alignment to be certain they haven't slipped. You can also use small clamps at this point, if you have them (see the bottom photo right). You only need a good glue joint, so don't apply too much pressure, which could cause the pieces to slip out of alignment.

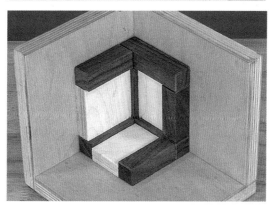

## Finishing the Puzzle

1 Use a sanding mop to give all the pent pieces a light sanding, which will make them slide together nicely. It's also important to sand the frame, especially on the inside edges.

2 Apply your finish of choice and then a coat of paste wax. Adding the wax so the pieces slide easily against one another is an important step as you must allow for the numerous wrong combinations that may be tried by the solver.

**You can use small** clamps to attach the final side of the frame.

# CAGED KNOT

*by Tom Jolly*

he Caged Knot is one of Tom Jolly's early designs, and he considers it his favorite. It's one of my favorites, too. While it seems fairly simple (three basic shapes that are inserted into a cage with no internal baffles or dead ends), it is anything but. This puzzle requires 13 moves just to take out the first piece. (Note that puzzles are usually presented to a solver assembled.) Another great feature of this puzzle is that it is expandable. Making slight modifications to the three board pieces can result in many variations on the same theme. I will cover only one version here, but

## WHAT YOU NEED

- Approx. 48 in. of ⅝-in. stock for the cage
- Approx. 36 in. of ⅝-in. stock for the inside pieces
- Crosscut sled
- Set-up bars or blocks
- Dial calipers
- 45° miter sled
- Long edge-beveling jig
- Wood glue
- Corner-gluing jig
- Large flat-gluing jig

| PARTS LIST | | | |
|---|---|---|---|
| SIZE | WALNUT | RED OAK | DIMENSIONS |
| 5-unit pieces | 12 (see text for further explanation) | 3 | $\frac{5}{8}$ in. x $\frac{5}{8}$ in. x $3\frac{1}{8}$ in. |
| 3-unit pieces | | 1 | $\frac{5}{8}$ in. x $\frac{5}{8}$ in. x $1\frac{7}{8}$ in. |
| 2-unit pieces | | 3 | $\frac{5}{8}$ in. x $\frac{5}{8}$ in. x $1\frac{1}{4}$ in. |
| 1-unit pieces | | 8 | $\frac{5}{8}$ in. x $\frac{5}{8}$ in. x $\frac{5}{8}$ in. |

put yourself to the test and see if you can come up with another variation.

With this puzzle, you are going to have the opportunity to try something new in building the cage. While you could build it using the same method described in the Twin Pentominoes into a Light Box puzzle (see p. 80), you will be building a box with mitered corners, which is a bit of a challenge. If you do not have an accurate miter sled (see the sidebar on p. 88), I suggest you use the butt joint method shown for the Twin Pentominoes puzzle.

## Cutting the Pieces

1 Using the crosscut sled, begin by cutting the walnut pieces for the cage to just slightly over 5 units long. A 5-unit piece from $\frac{5}{8}$-in. stock would be $3\frac{1}{8}$ in., so a $3\frac{1}{4}$-in. piece will work. You may be wondering why we are cutting these pieces square only to miter them later: Why not just miter them right from the beginning? Well, these are the extra cuts I refer to in the sidebar on p. 88. Because the miter sled cuts only one side of the miter and you are using a stop block for that, it avoids a lot of switching

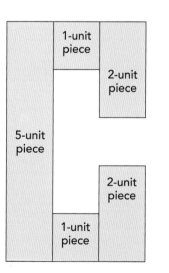

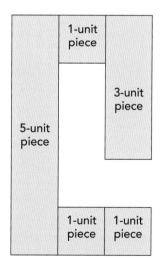

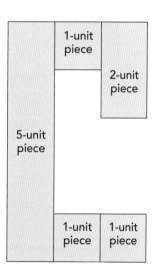

# THE 45° MITER SLED

Most miter sleds have two fences set at 45° so you can cut miters on both sides of the sled. Mine has only one fence and cuts miters on only one side. The reason I prefer this design is that it allows me to make my angled cuts downhill on the grain, which gives me a smooth cut with none of the fuzz on the trailing edge. It means a bit more work (a few extra cuts) and requires that the jig be made to cut a very accurate 45° angle, but I prefer to make my jigs do just one thing. That way, the jig is always set to do the same process without any adjustments.

**Use a stop block** with the miter sled to cut the frame pieces to a consistent length.

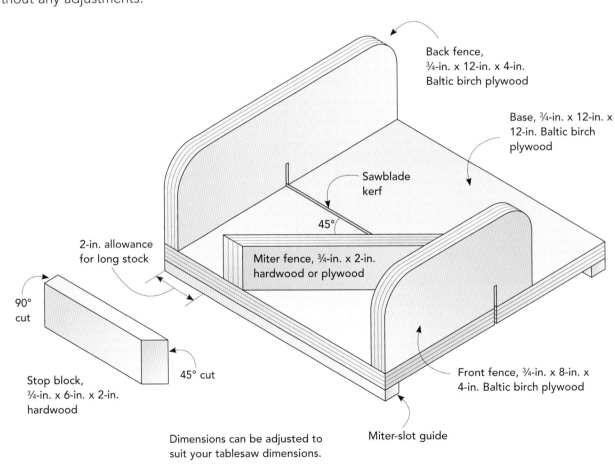

Back fence, ¾-in. x 12-in. x 4-in. Baltic birch plywood

Base, ¾-in. x 12-in. x 12-in. Baltic birch plywood

Sawblade kerf

45°

2-in. allowance for long stock

Miter fence, ¾-in. x 2-in. hardwood or plywood

90° cut

45° cut

Stop block, ¾-in. x 6-in. x 2-in. hardwood

Front fence, ¾-in. x 8-in. x 4-in. Baltic birch plywood

Miter-slot guide

Dimensions can be adjusted to suit your tablesaw dimensions.

back and forth between sleds or, even worse, adjusting your stop block on the miter sled. These joints are rather precise, and you want to set the stop block and not touch it until all the parts are cut.

2 Now cut the pieces for the three burr parts of the puzzle. (Note that these pieces should be accurate in length, not cut oversized like the cage pieces.) Follow the Parts List to see what you need to cut and the map for gluing up the pieces. Because these pieces will be sliding inside the frame and inside each other, I strongly recommend that you bevel the edges. Using a few extra pieces for spacing will help the pieces to fit together better.

3 Go back to the frame pieces and cut the miters on the miter sled. Place a stop block about 3¼ in. from the blade and secure it to the miter fence with a spring clamp or two. Clamp the frame piece to the fence and make your cut as shown in the second from bottom photo at right. Rotate the piece 90° and make another cut to end up with a piece as shown in the bottom photo at right. Cut all of the remaining frame pieces this way (you will need at least 11 more) before moving on to cut the other ends.

**Cut the red oak** pieces for the three burrs that go inside the cage. Use spacers to help align and fit the pieces during glue-up.

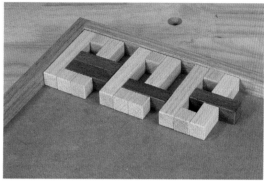

**Make the first** miter cut on the end of a frame piece. Be certain your clamp is far enough away from the blade.

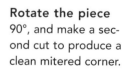

**Rotate the piece** 90°, and make a second cut to produce a clean mitered corner.

+
**TIP**

**The inside of the frame** and the consistency of the frame openings are important, so it may be helpful to use a piece of plywood, cut to size, when gluing the frames, as you did with the Twin Pentominoes puzzle (see pp. 83–85).

**Mark the frame** piece for the next mitered cut.

**The frame piece** should look like this when all four miters have been cut.

4 Mark the distance needed for the inside of the frame (1⅞ in.) on one of the pieces, as shown in the top photo at left. Make sure you are cutting the same two sides of the frame piece that you cut previously. Check the inside of the frame after making your first cut and adjust as necessary. If it is too long or too short, you will need one of those extra pieces I often refer to. When completed, your piece should look like the one shown in the bottom photo at left.

# Gluing Up the Frame

Now for the challenging part of this puzzle— gluing up the frame. I have experimented with many different approaches to the glue-up, including (a) gluing up two complete halves and then gluing them together and (b) adding one piece at a time, waiting for the glue to dry each time before proceeding. What works best for me, however, is to glue up two frame ends and then connect them with two legs at a time. You will see what I mean by this in the upcoming photos.

## CUTTING DOWNHILL

When cutting unusually shaped parts for a puzzle, there are many things working against you: blade deflection, fuzzy cuts/tearout, or a lack of precision. If you only cut downhill through the grain, you will notice a significant difference between each half of the cut. Your downhill pieces should be smooth and free of any fuzz or tearout, whereas the uphill piece (the cutoff) may not be as smooth. It's also a good idea to use a slow feed rate when cutting. Allow the blade to do the work. A faster feed rate can cause the blade to deflect and change the angle of your cut.

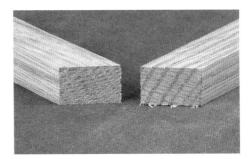

**Here's an example** of a cut made on the miter sled. The piece on the left is the downhill piece and the piece on the right is the uphill piece.

1 Begin by gluing the first two frame pieces together as shown in the top photos at right. I like to use the large flat-gluing jig for this, as I can see the glued piece a little easier than with the corner-gluing jig. Place these pieces face-down so that the outside of the frame is facing up, which ensures that the inside of the frame is flat and true. The outside of the frame is much easier to sand flat later, if necessary.

**Glue one face** of the mitered end.

**Apply firm**, steady pressure to get a good bond.

**The top and bottom** squares of the frame are glued up and ready to be connected by the side legs.

**Carefully remove** any glue from the valley of the miter joint.

**If necessary,** remove a small amount of stock from the center of the miter to allow for any glue that was not removed in the previous step.

2 Continue around the end frame until you have two squares as shown in the photo above. After these frames have dried, check for any squeeze-out (which would prevent you from getting a secure joint in the next step). Squeeze-out is easily removed with a sharp chisel. You can also shave a bit off the edge of your miter joint as necessary.

3 Switch to the corner-gluing jig, and lay one of the frames in the corner. Add one of the legs by applying glue to both sides of the miter and sliding it into place. Be sure that the leg seats fully in place and that the end frame is still snug in the corner. Allow this assembly to dry before adding the next leg.

**With one of the frames** flat in the corner jig, work your way around and add the legs.

**As every wood-worker** knows, you can never have too many clamps. Set the end frame on top of the four legs and use as many small clamps as necessary to pull the frame together.

**Sand the outside** of the frame with a random-orbit sander.

4 After you've added all four legs, let the assembly dry thoroughly. Then apply glue to the four corner miters and set the end frame onto the legs. Use several clamps to pull the frame together and remove any gaps that may be present due to a slight misalignment.

5 Once the frame has dried, sand it with a random-orbit sander to remove any irregularities in the frame sides. I must admit that my first few frames were not finished without needing some wood filler in a few of the gaps I created.

## Finishing the Puzzle

Finish the puzzle with a hand sanding or sanding mop to soften all the edges. Be sure to relieve the edges of the frame a bit, both inside and out. A coat of lacquer and a liberally applied coat of wax should soon have you scratching your head trying to put together this challenging puzzle. (The solution is presented on p. 157.)

## Tom Jolly

Tom, a retired electrical and astronautical engineer, got started designing puzzles when he was first exposed to a puzzle-designing software program. After posting a few of his designs to a popular puzzle website, several craftsmen sought permission to manufacture them. Encouraged by the interest in his designs, Tom has since created about 80 puzzles, of which about 35 have been produced by various companies and craftsmen.

The Caged Knot is Tom's favorite design. Outwardly, it appears rather simple to solve, but it has several dead ends and a tricky solution. What encouraged me to reproduce this puzzle myself was its simplicity of design and the complexity of solving.

Tom currently resides in California and is an award-winning board-game designer with more than a dozen published games (www.jollygames.com). He has also written a few short stories and fantasy stories that have made it to print.

# BUNDLE OF STICKS JR.

*by Tom Jolly*

T his puzzle is another design from Tom Jolly and one that's quite different from the others both in appearance and concept. It's a five-piece, simple but ingenious design. The idea is to thread the four sticks through the small frame, but the catch is that the sticks have several barriers attached to them. This is an easy puzzle to make with relatively few pieces and only one area where dimensions are critical. Solving it, though, is a different matter entirely. (The solution is presented on p. 159.)

## PARTS LIST

| SIZE | WALNUT | RED OAK | DIMENSIONS |
|------|--------|---------|------------|
| 7-unit piece | | 1 | ⅝ in. x ⅝ in. x 4⅜ in. |
| 6-unit piece | | 2 | ⅝ in. x ⅝ in. x 3¾ in. |
| 5-unit piece | | 1 | ⅝ in. x ⅝ in. x 3⅛ in. |
| 3-unit piece | 4 | 1 | ⅝ in. x ⅝ in. x 1⅞ in. |
| 2-unit piece | | 1 | ⅝ in. x ⅝ in. x 1¼ in. |
| 1-unit piece | | 11 | ⅝ in. x ⅝ in. x ⅝ in. |

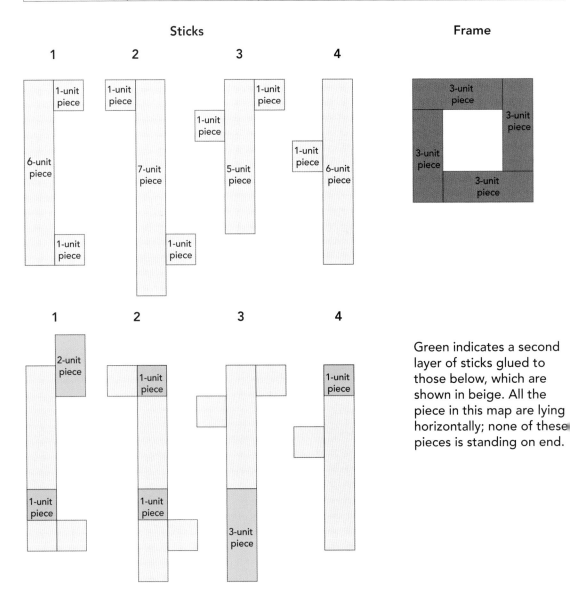

**Sticks**

**Frame**

Green indicates a second layer of sticks glued to those below, which are shown in beige. All the piece in this map are lying horizontally; none of these pieces is standing on end.

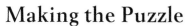

## WHAT YOU NEED

- Approx. 32 in. of ⅝-in. stock (red oak) and 14 in. of ⅝-in. stock (walnut)
- Crosscut sled
- Set-up bars or blocks
- Dial calipers
- Long edge-beveling jig
- Wood glue
- Large flat-gluing jig

## Making the Puzzle

1 Cut all the pieces to length and then bevel the edges of the red oak pieces (the sticks). I wait to bevel the walnut pieces until they are glued up into the finished frame.

2 Follow either the gluing map or the photo at right to make the sticks. Use spacers as necessary between the barrier pieces on the sticks to get the proper spacing.

3 The frame is simply glued end-to-side in a circular pattern. Use a few extra pieces as spacers to make sure that the frame is wide enough to accommodate all four sticks. You may find you need to sand out the center of the frame a bit so that the sticks can slide through it easily. It is easier to sand the inside of the one assembled frame than it is to sand all four sticks.

4 For appearance only, bevel the outside edges of the frame using the long edge-beveling jig. The sticks are best sanded with a sanding mop to soften the edges. Make sure that after finishing, you give the frame a good coat of wax.

**All the pieces are** cut and ready for glue-up: red oak for the sticks and walnut for the frame.

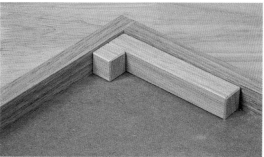

**The large flat-gluing jig** works well for this puzzle. Flip the sticks back and forth from side-to-side as you add the barrier pieces (the pieces that stick out).

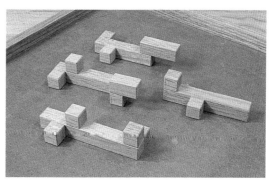

**The four glued-up sticks.**

**Glue up the four** walnut pieces for the frame end-to-side, as shown in the gluing map on the facing page. Use spacers in the center of the frame to ensure that it will accommodate the bundle of sticks.

# MURBITER'S CUBE

## by Primitivo Familiar Ramos

**M**urbiter's Cube is a puzzle that, while not too difficult to solve, requires a bit more skill to make. "What could be so difficult about this?" you may ask. Well, all of the eight finished pieces are identical. That may not seem like a big deal, but it also means that all the pieces are interchangeable. Every piece must be able to fit comfortably within any of the other pieces.

Don't be discouraged, though. With a little care when milling and cutting your stock, you should be able to make a nice-fitting puzzle.

An interesting feature of this puzzle is that it can be assembled into two different shapes: a 4 x 4 x 4 cube or an 8 x 4 x 2 brick. In each case, there are three possible solutions (one solution for each of the two shapes is presented on p. 160).

Another distinguishing feature of this puzzle is the way the edges are beveled. I recommend adding a slightly larger bevel to the edges, which will help in fitting the interchangeable pieces. You can easily make a new jig to accommodate the wider bevel, or, if you're working with the manual-style edge-beveling jig (see p. 25), you can use it on the largest setting by not adding any tape to the underside.

| PARTS LIST | | |
|---|---|---|
| SIZE | QUANTITY | DIMENSIONS |
| 4-unit piece | 8 | ⅝ in. x ⅝ in. x 2½ in. |
| 2-unit piece | 16 | ⅝ in. x ⅝ in. x 1¼ in. |

## WHAT YOU NEED

- Approx. 44 in. of ⅝-in. stock
- Crosscut sled
- Set-up bars or blocks
- Dial calipers
- Edge-beveling jig
- Wood glue
- Corner-gluing jig

**The pieces for** Murbiter's cube (left) have a wider bevel than normal (right), which helps the tight-fitting pieces slide together more easily.

**All the pieces** are ready to be glued into the eight identical parts.

**Test-fit the pieces** to make sure they can be assembled in a variety of ways without needing any force.

**Each part consists** of a 4-unit piece glued atop two 2-unit pieces.

## Making the Puzzle

1 The pieces for this puzzle are so simple that a map is not necessary. Simply cut 8 pieces that are 4 units long and 16 pieces that are 2 units long. Bevel the edges and you are ready to begin glue-up.

**Use two extra** pieces as spacers to ensure a good fit when assembling.

2 Each piece consists of one 4-unit piece and two 2-unit pieces, glued together as shown in the second from the top photo at left. Place two 2-unit pieces in the corner-gluing jig with two spacers in between, and apply glue to the far ends of the 4-unit piece before setting it on top of the 2-unit pieces. The space between the two "legs" of the piece needs to accommodate a two-unit piece when assembled. Continue gluing up the remaining pieces until you have all eight pieces for the puzzle.

**Place a 2-unit piece** in the corner-gluing jig followed by two spacers and another 2-unit piece. Add a little glue at each end of the 4-unit piece, and place it on top of the pieces in the jig.

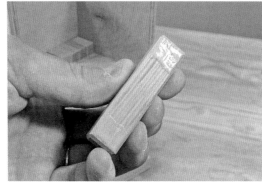

3 Allow the pieces to dry, then use a mop sander in the drill press for final prep before finishing. An application of finish and mandatory waxing will help you find all the possible solutions to this clever puzzle.

# TRIUMPH

## *by Stewart T. Coffin*

This classic Stewart T. Coffin design is a staple in every puzzle collector's collection. It is simple (with only six identical pieces), yet the confusing shape of the pieces makes it seem difficult. In the end, the solution (given on p. 162) is likely to cause you to slap your forehead and exclaim, "That's it?"

Another interesting feature of this puzzle design is that it has a few different solutions,

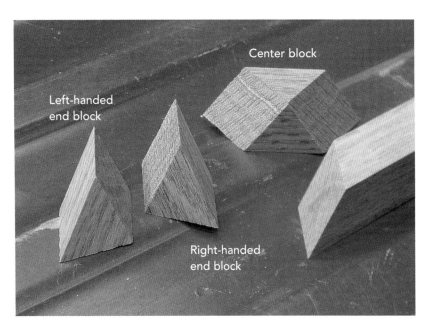

Center block

Left-handed
end block

Right-handed
end block

**For this puzzle,** you need to cut six 6-sided center blocks from ⅞-in.
stock, six left-handed end blocks, and six right-handed end blocks.

**TIP**

**When cutting the six-sided center block**
on the tablesaw, don't hold the offcut piece
with a clamp, which would force it down and
diagonally into the blade. Instead, use tape to
secure the offcut piece to the stop block.

## MAKING ADJUSTMENTS FOR THE
## SIX-SIDED CENTER BLOCK

If the middle point of
the center block looks
like this . . .

. . . move
stop blocks
closer to the blade.

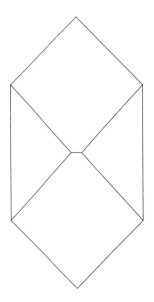

. . . move
stop blocks
farther from the blade.

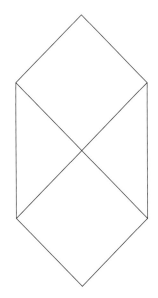

. . . perfect!

which make different shapes. Two are shown in the photos on p. 99. Play around with the pieces and see what other shapes you can come up with.

# Cutting the Parts

Start with about 36 in. of ⁷⁄₈-in. stock using the diagonal cutting jig (see p. 29). This puzzle will not require that much stock, but you'll likely make a few test cuts that may be inaccurate and cut a few parts that may just be flat out wrong! The 36 in. also includes the stock for the stop block.

1 Start by cutting the stop block for the diagonal cutting jig. Lay a piece of ⁷⁄₈-in. stock in the jig on the left side of the blade with the full thickness of the stock passing beyond the saw kerf, as shown in the top photo at right. After cutting through the stock and discarding the cutoff, trim the stop block down to 5 in. to 6 in. (with a 90° end), using the crosscut sled.

2 Place the stop block in the jig as shown in the center photo at right, and bring the point of the block up to where it just barely touches the sawblade. Secure the stop block with one or two of the clamps, and lay the stock for the center blocks in the jig so that it is just touching the stop block. Secure the stock with a clamp.

3 You can now cut your first six-sided center block. The stock you are cutting should touch the blade where the end of the angled cut falls. Make your first cut, and shut off your saw to check this piece for accuracy. You need to see a well-aligned point in the middle of the six-sided center block. If there is not an exact convergence of all four lines to a center point, you need to adjust the stop block and make a new cut (see the drawing on the facing page). Once you have the stop block set correctly, you can

**Position the ⁷⁄₈-in.** stock in the diagonal cutting jig, and make the first angled cut for the stop block.

**The stop block** (painted red for clarity) is in position for cutting the six-sided center blocks.

**To cut the first** six-sided center block, use tape to hold the cutoff in place—don't clamp it.

**Rotate the stop** block 90° to cut left-handed end blocks.

**The two-part stop** block. The longer part (with each end cut at 90°) is held down with a clamp. The shorter, walnut part (which is angled on one end) gets removed after setting up the cut. Adding a piece of UHMW plastic to the end of the square stop block helps it endure the frequent bumping that it receives.

**Set the stock** for the right-handed end block so that the angled cut on the end of the stock is just to the left of the saw kerf.

**Lay the removable** part of the stop block onto the stock, and snug the square stop block up against it. Clamp the square stop block and remove the walnut stop block.

make the rest of your cuts for the six-sided center-block pieces by rotating the stock in the jig 180° and advancing it up to the stop block. You will need six center blocks, but cut one or two extra (of course).

4 Now cut the left-handed end blocks. Rotate the stop block 90°, move it to the position shown in the top photo at left, and make the cut. Once again, use tape (not a clamp) to hold the cut-off piece securely. Test your cut to see that the left-handed end blocks are sized correctly: The triangular sides of the end block and the six-sided center block should be exactly the same size. You need six end blocks, but cut one extra.

5 Finally, cut the right-handed end blocks. For this you should use a two-part stop block. We need the two-part stop block because the stop block sits in the jig in a way that would otherwise trap your cutoff under it, a potentially dangerous situation. With the two-part stop block, half of the stop block is removable; you remove it once the stock has been accurately placed, which allows the cutoff to fall away from the blade and be easily retrieved once the saw has stopped.

**TIP**

**When you use** the two-part stop block, one part is held firmly down to the jig and the part up against the piece being cut is removed just before making the cut. This allows the cutoff to fall away. I still recommend taping the offcut with this setup because the piece that has fallen aside could still make contact with the blade, if there were excess vibration or sudden movement of the jig.

Align the stock so that the saw kerf will pass just to the right of the angled cut you have left from cutting the six-sided center blocks. Clamp the stock in place, and lay the removable part of the stop block on the face of the stock; slide them together for a tight fit. You can clamp the removable part in place temporarily as you add the second part of the stop block (the piece with the square 90° end), slide it up against the removable part, and lock it down with a clamp. Now take out the removable part of the stop block and you are ready to make the cut. Add a piece of tape to the offcut piece to keep it secure after it is cut free. Check your piece for accuracy as before, then cut the remaining left-handed end pieces. You should now have all the pieces you need for the puzzle.

## Gluing Up the Pieces

1 Each piece of the puzzle requires one of each of the three blocks you cut. Begin by laying the center block on its side with the point facing you. Glue a right-handed end block to the end of the six-sided center block, as shown in the second from top photo at right. Use finger pressure to align the back edges of the two blocks. Next, add the left-handed end block in the same manner. Your finished piece should look like the block shown in the second from bottom photo at right. Check the bottom of the block for flatness and a smooth transition between the three glued pieces. Glue up the remaining five pieces.

2 Flat-sand the bottom of each piece and relieve the edges. The cuts, if made correctly, can result in very sharp edges. I like the crisp edges but not so much that it is uncomfortable to hold the pieces. Finish, wax, and you are done!

**These are the** 18 pieces you need for gluing up the puzzle pieces.

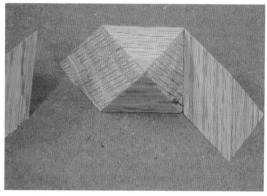

**A six-sided center** block has a right-handed end block attached.

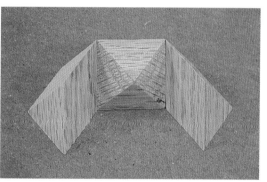

**The finished center** block should look like this.

**Examine the** bottom to check that all the pieces are flat and even. Sand lightly if necessary.

# VEGA

*by Stewart T. Coffin*

The Vega puzzle pieces bear a strong resemblance to those of the Triumph (see p. 99). Both these beauties have a six-sided center block as the base for the pieces, but the Vega introduces another rhombic shape into the mix: the tetrahedral block. Actually, this block is essentially just for visual interest, and you can make the puzzle without it and the solution is the same. Feel free *not* to add the tetrahedral block, if you would like to make a variation of this puzzle.

An accurate measurement of the amount of stock you need depends on how you cut the tetrahedral blocks. I like to use the diagonal cutting jig to cut the blocks, even though it creates some waste and you need to jump back and forth between setups. I favor wasting wood in the interest of safety, so I prefer not to cut from stock that is too small to be used safely with the diagonal jig. Therefore, I like to have plenty of extra stock and make all my cuts with one setup, change the setup, and then make the remaining cuts. More about this in the cutting section.

## Cutting the Parts

1 To begin, you need to cut 18 six-sided center blocks. For details on how to cut these, see the chapter on the Triumph (p. 99).

2 Before setting up to cut the tetrahedral blocks, I recommend that you take the pieces of ⅞-in. stock (about 6 in. long or longer) and cut the ends in the diagonal jig. This puzzle requires 12 tetrahedral blocks, so you need at least 6 pieces with both ends cut in the 45° jig to get the 12 pieces out. Set these angled pieces of ⅞-in. stock aside until after you've made the stop block.

3 For the stop block, you'll use the same square 90° piece used for the Triumph as the stationary part, but you'll make a different insert for the removable part. Make the insert by positioning a new piece of stock against the fixed portion of the stop block and clamping it

**Make two cuts** in the removable stop block (painted red for clarity) to create a 90° pointed end.

**Slide in the** contrasting wood for the tetrahedral blocks against the stop block and clamp the right side.

**Use a piece** of painter's tape to hold the cutoff piece in place alongside the stop block as you make the cut.

**The 18 six-sided** center blocks (in red oak) and the 12 tetrahedral blocks (walnut) are cut and ready for glue-up.

**Glue 3 six-sided** center blocks together as shown, one on each end of the center block in the middle.

down. You can then make your first cut. Next, rotate the stock 180° and make a second cut, creating a 90° pointed edge on the stock, as shown in the top left photo on the facing page. Leave this piece clamped in place, and remove any offcuts from the area. Once again, I have painted this stop block red for clarity.

4 Lay the angle-cut walnut stock against the stop block with the pointed end nearer to you as shown in the top right photo on the facing page. Clamp the right-hand piece down, secure the offcut with a piece of tape, and make the cut. You will need at least 11 more of these to give you the pieces as shown in the center right photo on the facing page.

## Gluing Up the Pieces

1 Position one of the six-sided center blocks on its side with the point facing toward you, and glue another six-sided center block onto each end as shown in the bottom photos on the facing page. This is similar to the way you glued the right- and left-handed blocks in the Triumph.

2 Add the tetrahedral blocks on each end to finish off the piece. The finished puzzle comprises six identical pieces.

3 Before doing any sanding, test-fit the pieces to see if any more aggressive sanding is required for a good fit. The Vega pieces usually have a tight fit, and sanding the flat or back sides of each piece will help.

4 Finish and wax the six pieces. (The solution is presented on p. 164.)

**The back side** of the three glued-together center blocks.

**The contrasting** wood of the tetrahedral blocks really adds some "pop" to the puzzle.

# DISTORTED CUBE

## by Stewart T. Coffin

This fascinating design from Stewart T. Coffin takes us in a new direction. For this puzzle, you'll be using the corner-cutting jig (see p. 27) to produce a number of truncated octahedrons. These shapes are fairly easy to make with a jig. Stewart actually references a jig that cuts off the eight corners of a cube to make the octahedron. I made my jig to trim off the 12 edges of a cube, which, while a bit more time-consuming, feels safer to me.

One of my favorite things about this puzzle is that it has several solutions. (Two of the variations are shown at right.) This is another design that almost begs you to try to experiment with other shapes to see if you can come up with something new. Stewart himself has spent a good deal of time experimenting with various polyhedral blocks and has come up with a few other designs not mentioned here.

## WHAT YOU NEED

- Approx. 16 in. of 1-in. stock
- Crosscut sled
- Set-up bars or blocks
- Dial calipers
- Corner-cutting jig
- Wood glue
- Large flat-gluing jig

**Be certain the cube** sits flat on the jig as you apply pressure with the clamp.

**Apply enough** pressure to hold the cube firmly in place. The rubber end of the clamp should be centered on the end of the cube.

**Make the first cut.** Notice the direction of the grain: You will get much better results if you always position the cube in the corner-cutting jig with the grain direction angling downward toward the blade. This is another example of cutting downhill on the grain.

**Rotate the cube** around the long-grain axis so you can make the rest of the cuts downhill.

**These three cubes** show the progression of cuts: the first four cuts (left), the next four (center), and the finished cube (right).

# Cutting the Cubes

All you need to make this puzzle are fourteen 1-in. cubes, but I strongly recommend that you cut a few extra cubes: If you are going to make a mistake, this is probably where it will happen.

1 Using the crosscut sled, cut your stock to accurate 1-in. x 1-in. x 1-in. cubes.

2 Using the corner-cutting jig (see the sidebar on the facing page), position one of the cubes and adjust the clamp so that it applies enough pressure to hold the cube in place securely.

3 Make the first cut, then rotate the cube so that the grain is in the same orientation. Make the other three cuts on this first cube.

4 After making these first four cuts, stand the cube up so that the grain runs vertically, which will give you a smooth, clean cut. Rotate the piece to make two vertical-grain cuts. To make the remaining six cuts to this cube, you'll need to adjust the clamp because the cube will now be a bit smaller and not fit with the current clamp setting. So make these first six cuts on all the remaining cubes, remembering to cut a few extras.

5 After adjusting the clamp for the new cube dimension, make the remaining cuts on each cube. You will notice that the cube does not have a very wide base to stand on as the sides are cut off. For this reason, it is important to make sure the cube is seated firmly against the angled sides and base of the jig and the clamp has been adjusted to hold it in place. Remember you still want to cut downhill, so orient your cube correctly in the jig. The finished piece should look like the cube at right in the bottom photo at left.

# Gluing Up the Pieces

There are not many pieces to this puzzle, so glue-up is pretty easy. Let's first carefully examine one of the octahedrons. You will notice that it has six square faces and 12 hexagonal faces. You only glue together the hexagonal faces.

1 The first glue-up is to join three blocks together along their hexagonal faces, as shown in the top photo at right. Make two of these three-piece assemblies for this puzzle.

2 Now glue up three blocks into an L-shape, as shown in the center photo at right. You'll need two of these assemblies as well.

3 When the assemblies are dry, position one of each on the gluing jig, as shown in the bottom photo at right (no glue at this point). Then add one of the remaining blocks to the empty space in the rear of the assembly, again without gluing it to either piece.

**Glue three cubes** together along their hexagonal faces; note that the pieces are oriented so that the glue joints are long grain to long grain. Make two of these assemblies.

**Glue up two** L-shaped assemblies.

**Begin assembling** the pieces for the bottom layer.

## CORNER-CUTTING JIG

The corner-cutting jig is used to cut the pieces for the Distorted Cube puzzle. You'll notice the letters "A" and "B" written on the jig. I often make notes on my jig about which sizes to use for which puzzles. This jig has two corner-cutting areas with different measurements. The A location is used for cutting 7⁄8-in. cubes and larger, and the B location is for cutting smaller cubes. I keep various-size cubes handy for reference.

**Add a single cube** to the empty space in the back row.

**Glue the remaining** L-shaped piece to the single cube on the bottom layer.

**Add the second** three-cube row to the pyramid, then dry-fit the last cube. If necessary to aid in final glue-up, mark the faces to receive glue with a small pencil mark.

**Glue in the last** cube and allow to dry.

4 You now need the second L-shaped assembly, which will be glued to the single piece you just added. Apply glue to the two inward-facing hexagonal faces of this single cube and place the L-piece on top of it, as shown in the second from top photo at left. You can place it in position and mark the faces that touch with a small pencil mark to be sure you apply glue to the right faces.

5 Set the second three-cube assembly at an angle, topping off the pyramid as seen in the second from bottom photo at left. The final piece gets glued to the angled piece you just added, by applying glue to the two appropriate faces and inserting it into the pyramid. Apply gentle pressure to all sides of this pyramid to ensure a good fit. If you cut your octahedrons accurately, there should be no gaps or mis-aligned pieces.

# Sanding and Finishing

The Distorted Cube is another good candidate for the sanding mop because the many faces of each piece make hand sanding impractical. Be careful with the sanding mop. It is easy to go overboard as the angles of these pieces are rather slight and easily rounded over. Add a little wax for that nice, soft feel, and see how many of the solutions you can come up with before looking at the answer on p. 165.

**The four finished** pieces should look like this.

# OCTAHEDRAL CLUSTER

*by Stewart T. Coffin*

W hen I first saw this puzzle design, it appealed to me for a couple of reasons. I liked the symmetry of the completed puzzle, which is easily enhanced by using various exotic woods, and, once taken apart, the puzzle has only four pieces. However, this can be a difficult puzzle to put back together. (The solution is presented on p. 166.)

This is another clever design that requires the use of the corner-cutting jig. The Octahedral Cluster also takes us a step further because it is interlocking, which not only makes the puzzle

## WHAT YOU NEED

- Approx. 24 in. of 7/8-in. stock for the puzzle; 16 in. of stock for the jig
- Crosscut sled
- Set-up bars or blocks
- Dial calipers
- Corner-cutting jig
- Wood glue

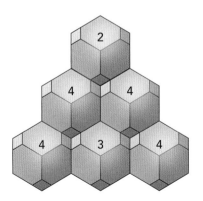

Bottom layer

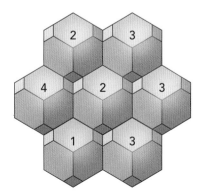

Middle layer

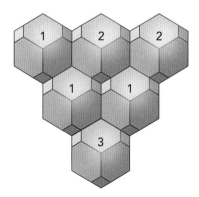

Top layer

a bit more confusing to solve but also adds to the difficulty when making it. But take heart, as with all of the puzzles in this book, the difficulty level is reduced greatly by careful milling and cutting of your stock. We will also be making a jig to help with the glue-up.

## Cutting the Cubes

To get started, you need to cut at least nineteen ⅞-in. cubes for the puzzle and twelve for the jig. These cubes will then be cut into octahedrons using the corner-cutting jig (see the Distorted Cube on p. 110 for instructions on this). Once you have all the cubes cut, you are ready to make the jig.

## Making the Glue-Up Jig

1 Begin by gluing together three blocks as shown in the top photo at right. Keep the grain direction running the same way, and glue only the hexagonal faces.

2 Continue with a second group of three, followed by a row of four and a row of two blocks.

**The first row** of the jig should look like this.

**These are the four** rows that make up the jig.

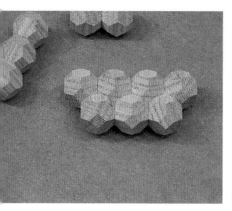
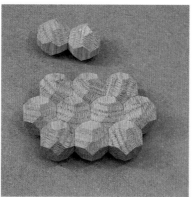

**To make the jig,** begin by gluing a row of four to a row of three (left), add another row of three to the row of four (center), and finally add the row of two (right). This is your finished jig.

**Glue together** the four #4 pieces for the bottom layer. (You'll notice that the jig appears a bit darker than the puzzle pieces because of the stain that was applied.)

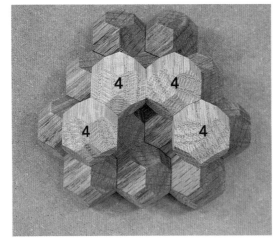

**Set pieces #2 and** #3 into the jig without glue; they will be glued to pieces on the next layer.

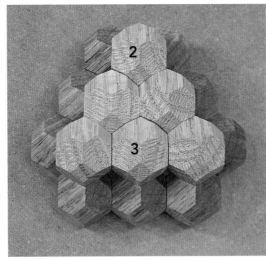

**Add the #2, #3,** and #4 pieces to the second layer.

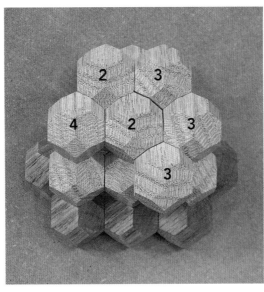

3 Glue the rows of blocks together by rotating each row slightly toward you so that you are again gluing the hexagonal faces together. Notice the orientation of the faces carefully. It's easy to glue the wrong hexagonal faces to each other. There should be a clear, repeating pattern as you go (see the bottom photos on p. 115).

# Gluing Up the Puzzle

Follow the map on p. 113 to glue up the puzzle pieces, laying the blocks into the jig as you glue. They should fit in the jig securely and snug up against one another. The tolerances for this puzzle are very tight; if you are not careful when gluing, you could wind up with an interesting-looking paperweight. Note that the numbers used in the map are for the order of the pieces in assembling the puzzle, not for gluing.

1 Begin by gluing together the four #4 pieces on the bottom layer.

2 After the #4 pieces have set up, add the #2 and #3 pieces, setting them in place without any glue.

3 Add the #2 pieces to the second layer, gluing the #2s together with the piece below. Continue with the #3 and #4 pieces, gluing them to the same numbered pieces. You will need to hold each of these pieces in place for a few minutes while they set up (you can use your fingers or a small piece of tape). Once you become familiar with how the pieces are glued up, you can build the subassemblies of each layer and add them as a unit, eliminating the

**TIP**

**Applying a stain** to the jig after glue-up helps make the pieces stand out a bit more. Also add a good coat of wax to prevent squeeze-out from sticking.

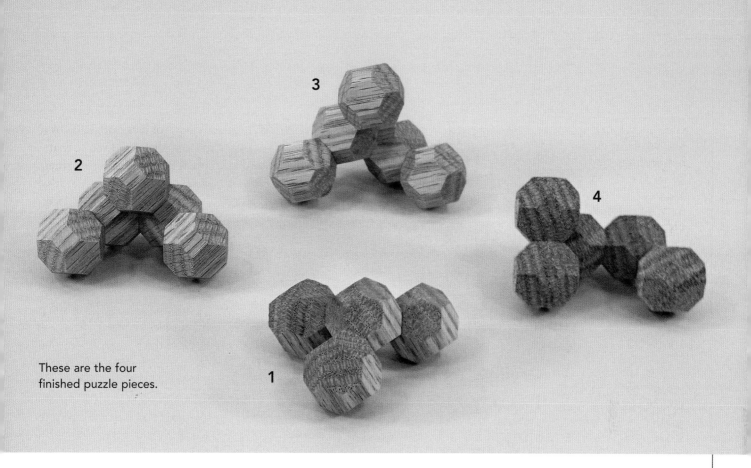

These are the four
finished puzzle pieces.

need to hold the parts until they dry. You will
add the #1 to the second layer when adding the
top-layer pieces. This way, you have something
to attach this block to.

4 Finally, add the top layer and slide the #1
piece from the middle layer up under the
other #1 pieces to help hold it in place.

If you see large gaps between the pieces,
apply light pressure to all sides to bring the
pieces snugly together before the puzzle is completely dry. Allow the puzzle to dry thoroughly
while it is sitting on the jig.

# Finishing

While this puzzle definitely needs some finish
and wax, it is important that you remove all
excess from the many inside corners of the puzzle. Excess wax can actually hold a puzzle
together, acting almost like a weak glue, and this
puzzle's irregular parts can be broken if too
much force is needed when solving.

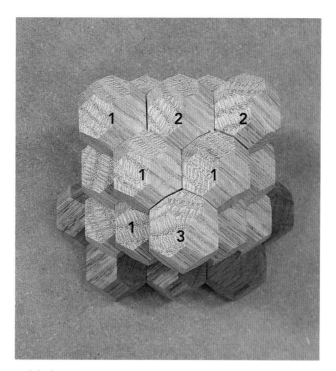

**Add the six pieces** in the top layer. The #1 piece from
the second layer can now be glued to the #1 pieces
above it.

# PEG PILE

*by Brian Menold*

This puzzle is one of my own designs. I was playing with a few pieces of wood that had a few holes in them, and I started thinking about how they could be used to create a puzzle. The Peg Pile is the result. While it may look easy, it is anything but. By my calculations, there are more than 4,000 incorrect ways to place the sticks (including mirrored solutions)—and only one correct way (see p. 167). If you use a different pattern of holes, you could come up with a puzzle that has multiple solutions, but I prefer just the one solution for this puzzle. As with most puzzles, the actual dimensions can be adjusted to suit your own taste. The only critical measurement is the alignment of the holes, which you'll do with the aid of a jig and a template.

## Making the Jig

For the Peg Pile, you first need to build a jig specifically for this puzzle and then build a tray for the puzzle pieces. The jig and accompanying template are used to accurately drill the holes in the six puzzle pieces. You might think you could just use the tray for this purpose, but you cannot. The jig requires higher sides to hold the pieces in place, and since you are drilling all the way through the puzzle pieces, you would wind up with a hole pattern in the bottom of the tray that gives away the solution.

1 Use the plan on p. 120 to cut all the parts for the jig from ¼-in. MDF or plywood. You'll need four sides, the jig bottom, and the hole template spacer. The only dimensions that are

### WHAT YOU NEED

- Approx. 4-in. x 16-in. x ¼-in. stock for the puzzle
- Approx. 4-in. x 12-in. x ¼-in. MDF or quality (flat) plywood for the jig
- 9 pegs (either store-bought or cut from wooden dowels)
- Drill press with ⁷⁄₃₂-in. brad-point bit (depending on pegs used)
- Crosscut sled
- Set-up bars or blocks
- Dial calipers
- Spray adhesive
- Wood glue
- Large flat-gluing jig

All pieces cut from ¼-in. stock

Puzzle pieces
1 in. x 3 in.

6
needed

Template
3 in. x 3 in.

Tray and jig bottom
3½ in. x 3½ in.

2
needed

Tray sides
3½ in. x
¼ in.

4
needed

Jig sides
3½ in. x
⅝ in.

4
needed

**Glue the first side** wall of the jig to the jig bottom. The wall should be ⅝ in. high.

critical for the jig are the inside of the box and the hole template that fits securely inside.

2 Glue one of the side walls of the jig along one of the edges of the bottom piece, leaving about a ¼-in. gap at one end, and allow this to dry. Then align the hole template spacer with this first side wall and add the next side at the opposite end, as shown in the top photo at right. Add the third side in the same way, then lift out the hole template spacer and lay it half out of the box as shown in the center photo at right. (I do this because the spacer can be difficult to remove if the joints are tight or if there is any glue squeeze-out.) Finally, add the fourth side using the hole template spacer to give you the correct spacing.

3 Give the edges of the hole template spacer a light sanding, and check that it fits snugly into the box but can also be removed without much difficulty. Now apply the paper hole template to the spacer. You can copy and cut out the one in this book or make your own; adhere the paper template with spray adhesive (you don't want it to move). If you choose to make your own paper template, note that the holes are precisely placed in the center of each quarter of the -in. squares. This allows for possible wrong placement of the pegs (to confuse the solver).

**TIP**

For a strong glue joint, make sure you apply a good coating of glue to the jig parts, especially on the end grain of the MDF, which soaks up the glue quickly. After assembly, allow the parts to dry thoroughly and test the finished assembly to be sure you have a secure bond.

**Align the template** spacer with the open end of the side wall you just glued and continue adding the second and third sides of the jig by butting each up against the previously glued side.

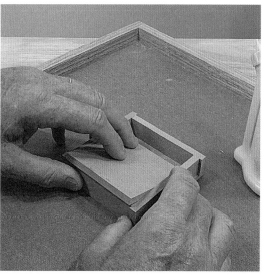

**Release the spacer** partway out of the jig so that it can be used for setting the fourth side wall.

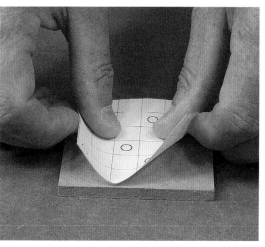

**Use spray adhesive** to adhere the hole template to the spacer.

**For the pegs,** you can use store-bought pegs (right) or make your own from lengths of wooden dowel (center).

**Clamp the four** glued-up corners of the puzzle tray.

**Before drilling the** holes in the six puzzle pieces, test the fit of the two layers in the jig. As necessary, sand any pieces so that they fit snugly.

# Building the Puzzle

1 While the hole-drilling jig is drying thoroughly, you can move on to the puzzle itself. Cut all the pieces for the tray and the six 1-in. x 3-in. puzzle pieces according to the plan on p. 120. For the pegs, you can either cut wooden dowels or purchase small wooden pegs from any hobby store. I chose to use the store-bought pegs, as they are much less work and have the added benefit of a small knob on the top, which makes them look a bit fancier.

The tray for the puzzle has the exact same pieces as the jig; the only difference is the height of the side walls at $\frac{1}{4}$ in. I like to make the walls just high enough to contain the first row of puzzle pieces. If you make them any higher, you will have to turn the tray over to remove the pieces every time you choose the wrong layout. And, believe me, that will happen quite frequently!

2 Use the same method of gluing up the sides of the puzzle tray as you did for the jig, using the hole template spacer as a guide to glue the side walls to the tray bottom. After gluing up all four sides, I like to clamp the corners while everything dries.

### TIP

**If you choose** to create your own template, don't just drill random holes, which would make solving the puzzle easy. Standardized spacing is what makes this puzzle difficult, as the holes seem to line up many ways, even if the pieces are placed upside down.

3 Once the tray is dry, you need to do a test fit of the six puzzle pieces in both the finished tray and in the hole-drilling jig. Set the first layer of three pieces in the bottom of the tray/jig, then arrange the second layer of three on top of the first three at a 90° angle.

4 There's no need to trim the sides of the hole-drilling jig, but you will want to clean up the puzzle tray. Smooth out the sides and bottom of the tray by first trimming with a handsaw or bandsaw. Then use a belt sander or random-orbit sander to flatten everything out.

5 Move to the drill press and prepare to drill the holes through the puzzle pieces. Adjust the drill bit so that it just penetrates the bottom of the jig, which will ensure that you'll drill all the way through the pieces. Use a sharp brad-point bit to help eliminate tearout. Your drill bit should be only about $1/32$ in. larger than the diameter of your pegs. My pegs are $3/16$ in. in diameter and I used a $7/32$-in. bit.

6 Place the hole-drilling template over the two layers of sticks in the jig and begin drilling. If there is excess play in your jig, add a peg to each of the holes as you drill them, which will help to keep everything in alignment. Be sure to keep a firm hold on the jig and its contents. If necessary, use a clamp to hold the whole assembly in place.

7 After drilling all nine holes, remove the template and take out the six puzzle pieces. Give everything a final sanding, finish, and wax, and be prepared to struggle with Peg Pile. Your hole-drilling jig and template not only serve as your solution, but they should also last through many more production cycles.

**Set the depth of** the drill bit to go all the way through both layers of the puzzle pieces and just into the jig bottom. Using a brad-point bit helps eliminate tearout.

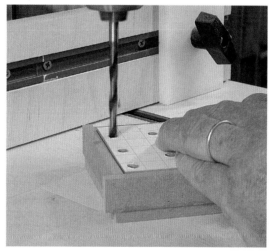

**Hold the template** atop the puzzle pieces in the jig as firmly as possible. Excess movement of the pieces can result in mismatched holes. A peg placed into the drilled holes will help keep things in alignment as you go along.

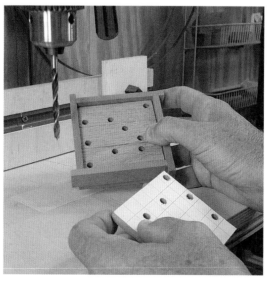

**A sharp bit gives** great results so the puzzle pieces should require little sanding. Keep the template as a reference for helping to solve the puzzle.

# CRUISER

## *by Stewart T. Coffin*

ere's a design for everyone who is tired of cutting all those strange shapes in the other puzzles. This one's a fabulous design made entirely from ¼-in. stock. Like all of Stewart T. Coffin's designs, the Cruiser looks rather simple . . . but is it? All you have to do is place the four pieces in the tray. It can't be that difficult. Well, it is when you don't have the solution in front of you. A really fun puzzle, this one will keep some folks baffled for days. Just always be sure to have it ready in its unassembled state.

## Cutting the Parts

Follow the plan on p. 126 to cut the four puzzle pieces that go in the tray. Give them enough of a sanding to bring them to final size. While this puzzle does not require as much accuracy as most of the others in this book, you still want to measure carefully. A bit too much play in the pieces can result in a puzzle that has solutions that are not intended. The dimensions for the tray are 3 in. x 4 in. You will be snugging the side walls up against the four center pieces.

**Cut the four puzzle** pieces that fit inside the tray. You'll need two of each size.

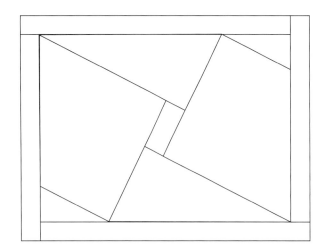

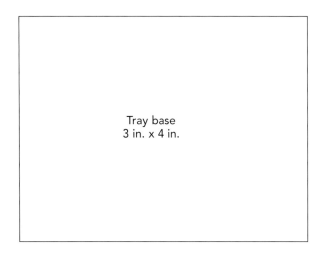

Tray base
3 in. x 4 in.

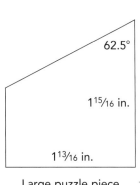

62.5°

1$^{15}/_{16}$ in.

1$^{13}/_{16}$ in.

Large puzzle piece
2 needed

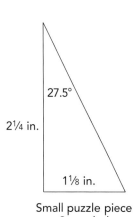

27.5°

2$^{1}/_{4}$ in.

1$^{1}/_{8}$ in.

Small puzzle piece
2 needed

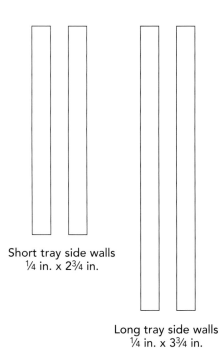

Short tray side walls
$^{1}/_{4}$ in. x 2$^{3}/_{4}$ in.

Long tray side walls
$^{1}/_{4}$ in. x 3$^{3}/_{4}$ in.

This will give you a good fit on the inside of the tray, and you can sand the sides of the tray smooth to remove the excess.

## Building the Tray

I like to construct a simple tray for this type of puzzle. You can certainly invest the time and energy in making something more elaborate with mitered corners and a floating bottom, but this puzzle will be played with a lot. I have even had some thrown in frustration! Practicality is more important than good looks here.

1 Tape the four puzzle pieces together in their solved state, and lay the assembly on the tray base. Using the same tray-building method that was used to make the Peg Pile (see p. 120), start by gluing one side wall along one long edge of

## WHAT YOU NEED

- Approx. 4-in. x 12-in. x ¼-in. stock (red oak)
- Crosscut sled
- Miter gauge for tablesaw, or bandsaw for cutting angled pieces (you can also use a small handsaw)
- Set-up bars or blocks
- Wood glue
- Belt sander
- Rubber feet (optional)

**With the puzzle** pieces taped together, glue one long side wall along one long edge of the base, keeping it approximately the width of one of the sides away from one edge.

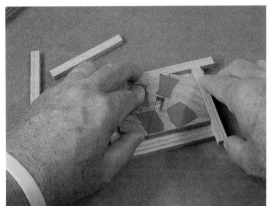

**Glue the adjoining** short side wall along the short edge of the base.

**Glue the last two** sides around the base, wrapping them around the four center pieces to ensure a snug fit.

**Glue small rubber** feet to the underside corners of the base.

the base. Then place the adjoining wall along the short side of the tray. Continue around the base to add the remaining side walls, being careful not to get any glue squeeze-out on the four pieces being used as spacers.

2 When the sides have dried, remove the four center pieces and the tape. Dry-fit the pieces back into the tray, and lightly sand to get a comfortable fit. They should be easy to remove but without too much play around the edges.

3 When the tray has dried completely, trim off most of the excess from the overhanging side walls (I use my bandsaw to do this). A trip to the belt sander makes quick work of smoothing out the sides, but be careful not to overdo it and make the sides uneven in thickness. After a thorough sanding all around (including the base of the tray), you are ready to apply the finish.

4 To give an extra nice touch to any puzzles I make with boxes or a tray, I like to add small rubber feet to prevent scratching any furniture and to give a good grip that keeps the puzzle from sliding around while trying to solve it. (See p. 167 for the solution.)

# TABULA CUBE

## by Yavuz Demirhan

The Tabula Cube was the first one of Yavuz Demirhan's designs that I made. I was drawn to what at first appeared to be a very simple design, but what a surprise when it came time to solve it! This puzzle is not only difficult to solve, but it also requires a great deal of dexterity to hold everything in place and make all the appropriate moves to get it back together. There are other designs similar to this by Yavuz and other designers as well. When made from contrasting or exotic woods, this style of puzzle really makes an impression. The glue-up is a bit tricky, and care must be taken to avoid squeeze-out while still getting good adhesion. But I think you'll find the Tabula Cube to be a fun challenge even for the serious puzzle solver.

This is also the first puzzle you will make that uses something other than the usual ⅝-in. or ¾-in. stick stock—in this case, some ⅛-in. flat stock. My wood supplier often only has a particular wood as 5/4 stock. I take this opportunity to resaw ³⁄₁₆ in. off the board to keep for puzzles such as this—especially when using exotic species. You don't want to add that extra wood to your dust collection system!

## Cutting Your Stock

1 Start by cutting the cubes to exactly ¾ in. x ¾ in. x ¾ in. You'll need 26 for the puzzle, but, as usual, cut a few extras.

**Prepare the stock** for the sticks (left) and the cubes (right).

## STICK DIMENSIONS

The sticks used in this puzzle are one exception to my emphasis on accuracy. While the width of the stick stock must match the width of the cubes, it is okay if the thickness doesn't match my dimensions exactly or if the sticks are *just a bit* long (1/32 in.). They will stick out beyond the side of the puzzle and can easily be sanded down with a random-orbit sander when the glue has dried. You will be adjusting the length of the sticks based on the width of the cubes plus their thickness. So if your sticks are more or less than 1/8 in. thick, adjustments for that will be made during cutting. Just be certain the thickness is consistent.

I prefer not to bevel the edges of the cubes for this puzzle. Remember that you also have the sticks in between the cubes, and they do not lend themselves to beveling the edges due to the thickness of the pieces.

2 Next, prepare the sticks that go between the cubes. If you are working with 3/4-in. stock, you can rip the sticks out to a rough 3/16-in. thickness and run them through a drum sander to bring them down to 1/8 in. The final thickness of these sticks is not as important as the fact that they are all the exact same thickness. You will see why when you glue up the puzzle. In the end, you want to wind up with 60 in. of stock that is exactly 3/4 in. wide by a consistent thickness of approximately 1/8 in.

**TIP**

**The Tabula Cube** is a puzzle that can be destroyed by squeeze-out. The tolerances are tight until you take it apart and give it a light sanding. If you find that a piece doesn't move after the glue has dried, tap one of the sides on a flat surface. Often there is only a small amount of glue holding a corner in place where it shouldn't.

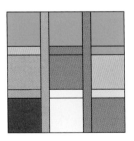

**Bottom layer**
Cubes and sticks

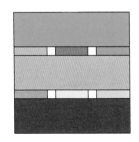

**Second layer**
Sticks

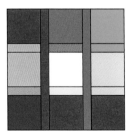

**Middle layer**
Cubes and sticks

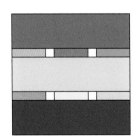

**Fourth layer**
Sticks

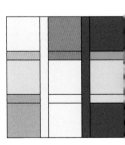

**Top layer**
Cubes and sticks

3 Now prepare to cut the sticks to length. Here is where you can make some adjustment to the length. Set the stop block on the crosscut sled using three of the cubes and two small pieces of the stock for the sticks, as shown in the top photo at right. Bring the stop block up to just touch the side of the pieces, but don't put any pressure on the pieces, which might cause deflection of the blade and will result in the sticks being too short. Remember, it's fine if the sticks are $\frac{1}{32}$ in. long, but no longer, unless you like sanding. After cutting a sample stick, check the length of the five pieces and compare it to the length of your stick; it should be the same, but I double-check all measurements to be sure. Once you are happy with the length, cut the remainder of the sticks. You will need 18.

## Gluing Up the Puzzle

Before you begin, thoroughly familiarize yourself with the gluing map shown on the facing page. Walk yourself through the steps of assembling the puzzle and how the pieces will be glued together. This can be a confusing glue-up. I still rely heavily on this map when I make these puzzles, and, yes, I still mess up occasionally.

I have shown this map with colors to differentiate the pieces as opposed to numbers. As there are two different-shaped pieces used in building the puzzle (sticks and cubes), it is less confusing. Note that some of the sticks run vertically, and you will need to work around them as they stick up above the bottom layers. I'll cover the gluing of the first layer in detail to get you started.

**To set the length** of the sticks, place three cubes and two pieces of the stick stock in the crosscut sled. Gently snug up the stop block against the cube at the end.

**Start the first row** with a green cube in the corner and an orange stick next to it.

**Add a gray cube** and a gray stick.

**Following the map,** the final cube in the first row is a red.

+
**TIP**

**Always err on** the side of *not* gluing. In other words, be certain that you are putting glue on the correct pieces. You can always go back and glue two pieces together that you missed, but you will not be able to undo the puzzle if you accidently glue up the wrong pieces.

**Add a horizontal** gray stick to the outside of the first row and glue it to the center cube of the first row.

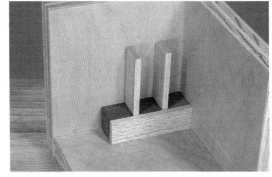

**The completed bottom layer.**

**Glue the first stick** in the second layer to the top of the three rear cubes. Be careful not to get any glue on the sticks in between the cubes; you are only gluing this horizontal to the cubes.

**The layer of sticks** is in place above the bottom layer.

1 Using the corner-gluing jig, begin by placing a cube in the corner (green on the map) and position a vertical stick (orange) against its front side without glue (see the second from top photo on p. 131). Place another cube (gray) in front of the vertical stick, and glue the next vertical (gray) stick to it. Add another cube (red) in front (without glue) to complete this row.

2 Before beginning the next row, add a horizontal stick (gray) and glue it to the center cube (gray) of the first row, as shown in the top photo at left. You may want to mark the area to be glued by placing the stick in place and making a small pencil mark where it meets each end of the center cube.

3 For the second row on the bottom layer, add a cube (green) and place a vertical stick (brown) in front of the cube. The next cube (brown) gets glued to that stick. Another vertical stick (yellow) with the last cube (yellow) in this row glued to it finishes the row (remember to follow along with the map at on p. 130). The next horizontal stick is added and glued to the center cube of this second row in the same way as the previous row.

4 Begin the final row of the bottom layer with another cube (green) and a vertical stick (green) glued together. Next, place a cube (orange) and a vertical stick (light blue) before adding the final cube (gray) and gluing it to the horizontal stick on its left. When completed, the bottom layer should look like the assembly in the second from top photo at left.

5 Now add the horizontal sticks that are placed flat on top of the cubes in the bottom layer (referred to as "Second layer: Sticks" on the map). The back stick (green) gets glued to the bottom-layer cubes.

The middle horizontal stick (orange) is glued only to the middle cube (orange) in that last row. Lastly, the front horizontal stick is placed on the front row and is glued to the near left cube (red).

5 At this point, we have completed the first two layers and the process continues in this same fashion. If you were able to follow the map up to this point, you should be comfortable proceeding. If not, review the map and take another try run by assembling the puzzle following the instructions and the map without any glue. As you go through the next few layers, take your time and pay close attention to excess glue and the relationship of the pieces to one another. Your finished cube should look like the one shown in the top photo at right.

## Sanding and Finishing

Once dry, the puzzle can be sanded in its solved state by either rubbing it in a circular motion on top of a piece of sandpaper or by using a random-orbit sander. This will even out the outside edges of the pieces all at once.

A light hand sanding of the individual pieces is necessary to soften the edges and to allow the puzzle to fit together better. (The eight finished pieces of the puzzle—and the solution for solving it—are presented on p. 168.) The tolerances for this puzzle are tight, so finish it off with a light application of finish and a necessary waxing.

**The completed** Tabula Cube is ready for sanding and finishing.

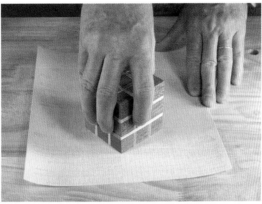

**Wrap your hand** around all four sides of the puzzle and move it in a circular motion on a sheet of sandpaper to even out the sides.

**If using a random-**orbit sander to sand the cube, take care not to apply too much pressure at the edges, which can cause a slight rounding over of the sides.

TIP

**Sometimes it may help** to glue a cube to a stick before trying to add it to the rest of the puzzle, especially if it is going toward the back of the gluing jig. If your puzzle is dry enough, you can also pull it away from the back of the jig and insert the piece before pushing it back and applying light pressure to get a good glue joint.

# TAKING YOUR PUZZLES TO THE NEXT LEVEL

There are many things that make someone want to pick up a puzzle and play with it. Aside from the actual design of the puzzle, these include the use of contrasting woods, color, pattern, figure, highlighting, or even cutting your wood at an angle. As you read through the ideas presented in this section, I'm sure you'll come up with a few design changes of your own.

Using alternating blocks of light and dark woods (here, oak and walnut) adds visual interest to a square-stock puzzle.

## Using Contrasting Woods

I have shown a few simple examples of ways to add interest to your puzzles in a couple of the designs in the book, such as the contrasting woods used for Little Kenny and Tabula Cube.

Look at the puzzle Little Kenny, at left, for example. The alternating blocks of walnut and oak serve no purpose, other than to make the puzzle a bit more interesting. It's easy to incorporate stripes or a checkerboard effect into a design, adding visual interest without a lot of work. Another way to use alternating woods is to place the contrasting wood blocks only on the corners for an entirely different look. I have even gone to the trouble of gluing up diagonally cut strips to create bicolored blocks that can make a multitude of unique patterns.

You know you can achieve nice results using red oak and walnut without breaking the bank. Now, how about adding a little maple into the mix? The addition of this third domestic wood can take the design up a notch. The deep brown of the walnut with the medium brown of the red oak and the beige or nearly white of the maple can be a great combination of woods. Using these three woods to create pattern gives you even more options.

The puzzle in the middle is the Five-Piece Solid Block featured in this book. It's a fun puzzle in its own right, but using exotic woods in two different patterns (left and right) makes for a more intriguing design.

## Incorporating Exotic Woods

Introducing exotic wood into your puzzle making opens up a whole new world of opportunities to get creative. The color and figure of many exotic wood species are simply stunning, and vibrant colors and vivid grain patterns can really add pop to any woodworking project. Deep, rich browns and subtle figure can add a certain elegance and class to a puzzle, which is why they are sometimes given as "executive gifts." I've seen many puzzles wind up on a coffee table or office desk, where they are used more as sculpture or decoration than as a puzzle to be solved. If a puzzle's only purpose is to be played with and subjected to abuse from weather, dirty hands, chewing by pets or children, and eventually losing pieces, then by all means stick to inexpensive woods. But if you desire a greater appreciation of your work, exotic wood choices can play a big part.

Using exotic woods to provide contrast is an excellent way to make your puzzle catch a person's eye, but be careful not to overuse exotics. While they are beautiful, exotic woods can be overwhelming when used to excess. I use exotic woods almost exclusively for the collectible puzzles I make, but I'm always careful when combining two or more exotic woods to allow one wood to showcase it and the others to play a backup role. For example, the use of something vivid, such as redheart, contrasts nicely with a dark wood such as ebony or wenge. I will even go to great lengths when using the wenge to hide the figured part of the face grain inside or to the sides of the puzzle. This gives you a nice contrast of the highly figured redheart against the dark and rather plain but complementary wenge.

### TIP

The way you use contrasting or complementary woods can give the solver a clue as to the orientation of each piece, if he or she knows that the puzzle is layered in different colors. This may result in a faster than normal solution for those you hope to fool.

**Another way** to add visual interest is to use a different species for each piece of the puzzle, as in this version of 8 Plaques = Cube.

## INTANGIBLES ADD APPEAL, TOO

When considering any material upgrade for a puzzle, make sure you use wood wisely and with a purpose. It should add something to the overall puzzle. Visual appeal, weight, feel, movement, and even sound are all elements of a wooden puzzle that people may notice. Your wood choices can add to or subtract from these elements. I once read a blog review of one of my puzzles, where the blogger mentioned the "very satisfying thwack" of the pieces as they slid together when he was attempting to solve it. Yes, even sound can play a part in the appeal of a puzzle!

**Here are two** examples of how exotics can improve the look of the Bedevil. On the left, the highly figured black palm wood is softened by the use of sycamore. On the right, using two bright colors makes the puzzle stand out.

**The high contrast** in the Vega puzzle on the left is more likely to catch the eye than the more restrained version on the right.

**The two beveled-**corner cubes in the foreground (bottom left photo) are the exact same shape but have a stunningly different effect. The beveled cube on the left was made from the red oak cube behind. The beveled cube on the right was made from a holly cube with thick yellow-heart and paduak veneer glued to each side before cutting.

**Sometimes it pays** to break all the rules. The seven pieces of this Convolution contain about 24 different species of wood. Over the top . . . or a unique design? You decide.

# Using Figure Effectively

The same rules apply with highly figured woods, whether domestic or exotic. I try not to mix two or more highly figured woods in most puzzle designs. While some combinations can be beautiful, I recommend that you err on the side of caution. However, I have successfully combined several different figured woods into one puzzle (as shown in the top photo on the facing page), but the object here was to make *each piece* out of a different exotic wood.

If you are in doubt about the look of a design, stack your pieces together before gluing up to see how they will look. It should give you an idea of how the final piece will look and whether you should try a different combination. Remember, when you're using exotic woods, experimenting can be expensive if the results are unattractive.

Figure should also be handled carefully, even when you're only using one species. What may look beautiful in an 8-in. x 6-ft. board may not translate well into a $^5/_8$-in. x $^5/_8$-in. x $^5/_8$-in. cube. Try to visualize the actual size you will end up

**These are four frames** for the Twin Pentominoes into a Light Box puzzle. The dark frame in the rear is the one featured in this book. The frame at left was made with sticks glued from half maple and half walnut, which gives the inside of the box a different color than the outside. The front frame was made by veneering the maple stock with an exotic on two sides; the corners were mitered and the edges chamfered to obtain the light beading on the edges. The frame at right was made with zebrawood cubes in the corners. None of these enhancements are difficult, just a little more time-consuming.

with before deciding to use figured wood. It must come across well in a much smaller size.

## Highlighting with Wood

Another way to add visual interest to your puzzles is by adding contrast or color to a puzzle in ways other than making the pieces out of different woods. This is somewhat difficult to explain because it is really a matter of using your imagination. The one thing to consider before trying anything new is that it usually requires more cutting, gluing, and sanding—in other words, more work. And you are still trying to maintain the same level of accuracy as with the simpler designs. The bottom left photo on p. 137 is a good example of introducing color or contrast for visual interest. I created a very different look to one of the cubes for the Octahedral Cluster

by gluing a few thin pieces of contrasting woods onto each of the six sides of a cube before cutting off the corners.

Some other ways to add interest are to use splines in boxes, trim on boxes, or laminations on almost anything. The photo above shows a few examples of how your puzzles can be enhanced with these techniques.

Now that you've seen some of the possibilities, the next step is to get your imagination going. See what ideas you can come up with to take your puzzles to the next level. Small additions or changes to a design can have a significant impact on the finished product. Don't be afraid to take chances, as puzzles use very little wood. Some of my nicer design modifications came about by just experimenting. I think you may surprise yourself. Enjoy!

# SOLUTIONS

# FIVE-PIECE SOLID BLOCK SOLUTION *(instructions for building the puzzle are on p. 36)*

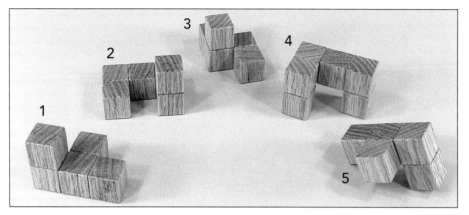

Identify the five pieces, which are numbered in the order of assembly. Notice the orientation of the pieces. If you aligned the grain of the wood when gluing up the puzzle, it should help you with the assembly.

**A**

Position pieces 1 and 2 as shown.

**B**

Slide pieces 1 and 2 together to form the base of the cube.

**C**

Place piece 3 on top of the base.

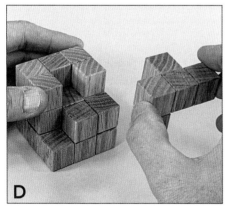

**D**

Piece 4 straddles the top of the pieces already in place and leaves the last space to be filled by piece 5, oriented as shown.

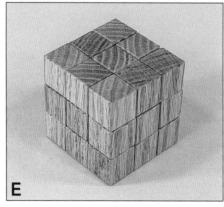

**E**

The final result is a finished cube that will baffle the uninformed.

# LITTLE KENNY SOLUTION *(instructions for building the puzzle are on p. 43)*

Little Kenny has only four pieces but is another sequential challenge. The pieces are numbered in order of assembly.

**A**

Holding pieces 1 and 2 as shown, slide them together. There should be an L-shaped hole when looking into the top of the assembly.

**B**

Insert piece 3 from the bottom, bringing it flush with the top of the first two pieces.

*(continued on next page)*

# LITTLE KENNY SOLUTION *(continued)*

Extra cube

The next step can easily go wrong if you are not careful. Piece 4 is a large contorted C-shaped piece that has one extra cube in one corner. Hold the piece with the extra cube facing you. Align the front leg of the C with the hole in the front of the three-piece assembly and insert it.

Slide up only pieces 1 and 2 from this assembly so that the puzzle looks as shown. Piece 4 can now slide to the right.

Push up on the piece sticking out of the bottom, and slide the piece on the right in to complete Little Kenny.

# THREE-PIECE BLOCK SOLUTION *(instructions for building the puzzle are on p. 48)*

The Three-Piece Block has the fewest number of pieces of all the puzzles in this book, yet it may be the most confusing. It is occasionally solved by chance but still remains a difficult puzzle, until you memorize the alignment of the pieces.

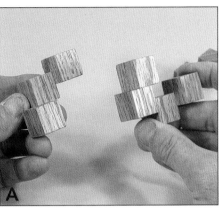

Take note of the differences in the two pieces made from three cubes. The easiest to identify is piece 3, which has two cubes with a common plane. In piece 1, all of the cubes are on different planes; in other words, none of the cubes are aligned in any way. Once you have the pieces identified, you can begin.

Holding pieces 1 and 2 as shown, bring them together so that there are three cubes aligned in a stair pattern facing you.

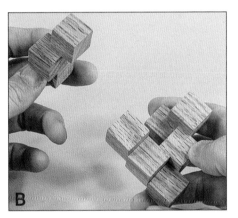

Holding this assembly in one hand and piece 3 in the other, place the offset cube between the gap on top of the assembly.

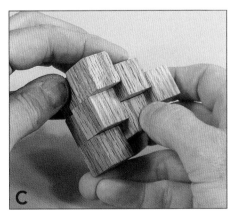

If you made your puzzle correctly, the pieces should fit snugly and the finished assembly should hold together when placed on a flat surface.

# CONVOLUTION SOLUTION *(instructions for building the puzzle are on p. 54)*

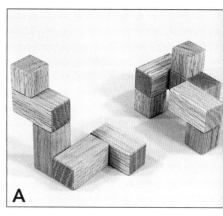

The Convolution is a sequential interlocking puzzle that can only be solved using the correct order of assembly. The pieces here are numbered in the order of assembly.

Position pieces 1 and 2 as shown.

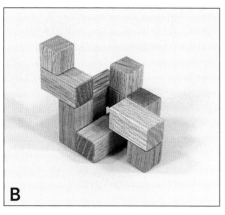

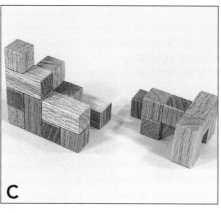

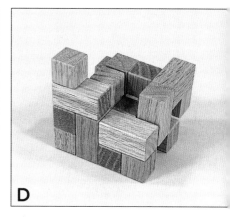

Lift piece 2 and place it over piece 1.

Slide pieces 1 and 2 together, and position piece 3.

Lift piece 3 and place it over the assembly as shown.

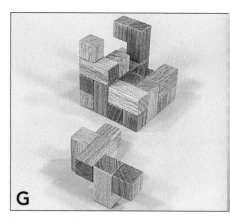

Piece 3 should drop down over the back leg of piece 1. Piece 4 is next.

Slide piece 4 into the back side of the assembly, completing the back corner.

Piece 5 is the tricky one, requiring a rotation. Begin by positioning the piece as shown.

**H**

lace piece 5 on top of the cube t the angle shown. It will only fit ne way.

**I**

Now you can rotate piece 5 clockwise, sliding its back leg under piece 4.

**J**

As you rotate piece 5, begin to slide it toward you as well, pulling it into its final position as shown. Next, position piece 6.

**K**

ift piece 6 and drop it into place n top of the cube.

**L**

Position piece 7.

**M**

ift piece 7 and slide it in from ne right, aligning the forward leg s shown.

**N**

That's it! Your Convolution is ready to frustrate your friends and family.

# THE ELEVATOR SOLUTION *(instructions for building the puzzle are on p. 59)*

These directions show the assembly of the Elevator. Since you glued up your Elevator in a completed state, you will have to follow these directions in reverse to get it apart the first time.

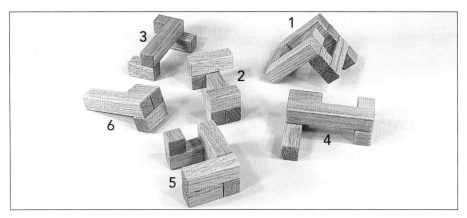

The pieces of the Elevator, shown here in order of assembly, require a few rotations. Follow the photographs carefully to make the rotations correctly.

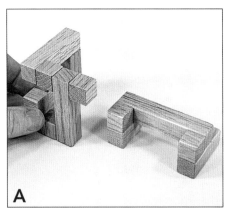

Align pieces 1 and 2, and insert the square end of 2 through the hole in piece 1.

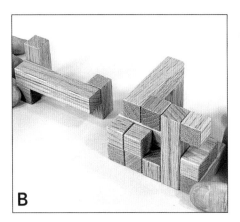

Let piece 2 drop down and slide it forward to wrap around piece 1. Piece 3 gets inserted from the left, through the L-shaped hole formed by pieces 1 and 2.

Once piece 3 has passed through the hole, slide both pieces 2 and 3 back. Slide piece 2 all the way to the left.

Insert piece 4 just to the left of piece 1, and slide it right until it rests against piece 1. While holding pieces 1 and 4 together, slide them both to the left.

Rotate piece 4 90° as shown. Bring piece 2 forward to fit around the base of piece 1.

(continued on next page)

# THE ELEVATOR SOLUTION (continued)

Slide piece 3 to the right while supporting piece 4. Rotate piece 4 once more, this time to the left.

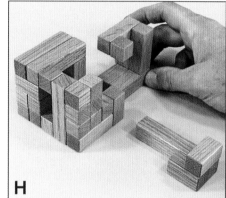

Once piece 4 has been fully rotated, slide it forward. Your puzzle should now be looking a bit more like the finished puzzle.

Insert piece 5 through the back.

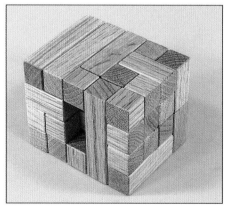

Slide the final piece (6) into the side as shown.

# SATURNO #1 SOLUTION *(instructions for building the puzzle are on p. 64)*

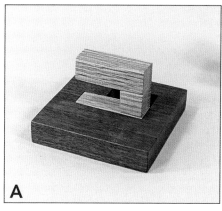

**A**

The Saturno #1 consists of the frame and three pieces, two of which are identical. They shouldn't create any confusion, so there's no need to number the pieces for this one.

Place the U-shaped piece into the frame as shown.

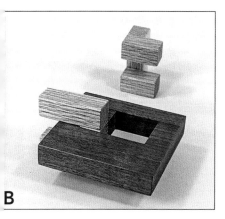

**B**

Drop the piece so that it can slide all the way into the left notch of the frame.

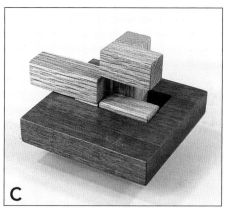

**C**

Insert one of the remaining pieces into the frame oriented as shown.

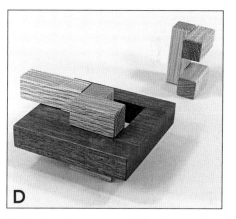

**D**

Slide the piece toward the front of the frame, creating an opening for the next piece.

**E**

Orient the final piece correctly and drop it into position.

*(continued on next page)*

Slide all three pieces to the right, allowing you now to slide the U-shaped piece to the rear of the frame.

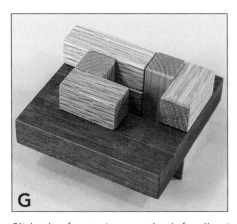

Slide the front piece to the left, allowing the back piece to come forward.

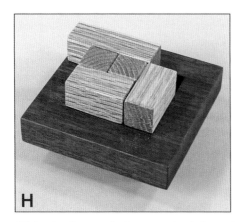
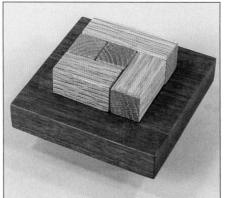

Slide the forward piece to the left and the U-shaped piece to the right, centering the three pieces in the frame.

# 3 PLAQUES = CUBE SOLUTION *(instructions for building the puzzle are on p. 67)*

Except for pieces 1 and 2, there is no particular order of assembly for this puzzle. These two pieces are inside the cube and need to be put together first, but the remaining pieces can be placed in any order.

Holding pieces 1 and 2 as shown, insert piece 2 into piece 1 and slide them together.

**B**

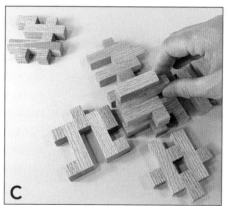

**C**

Here I have arranged the pieces as if the sides were unfolded from the cube. The top piece (3) is in the upper left and I am holding the piece 1-2 assembly in my hand.

Begin by placing the piece 1-2 assembly into piece 6, which is now the bottom of the cube.

*(continued on next page)*

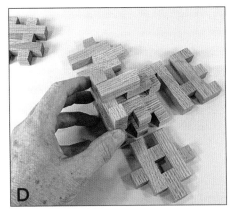

Now you can simply stand up the remaining four sides. If positioned correctly, they will fit nicely, leaving only the top piece (3) to finish off the cube.

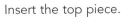

Insert the top piece.

The completed cube.

# KNOTTY 3 SOLUTION *(instructions for building the puzzle are on p. 71)*

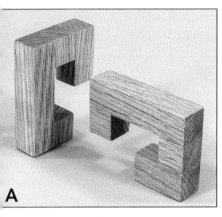

**A**

All three pieces of the Knotty 3 are identical. Start with any two and position them as shown.

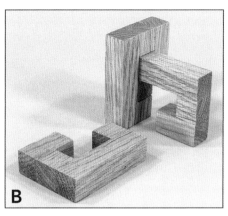

**B**

Insert the right piece into the left piece but not all the way through. You need to leave a space for the third piece to be inserted.

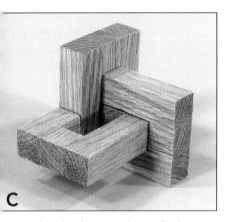

**C**

Insert the third piece through the second piece.

**D**

Slide the second and third pieces to the left as one.

**E**

Slide the third piece forward to finish the assembly.

# BEDEVIL SOLUTION *(instructions for building the puzzle are on p. 74)*

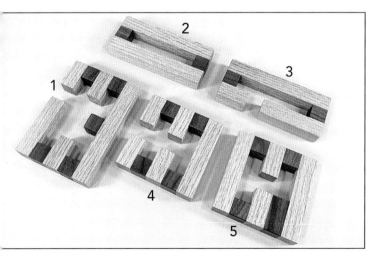

The five pieces of the Bedevil are all unique. Here, they are numbered in the order of assembly.

*(continued on next page)*

# BEDEVIL SOLUTION *(continued)*

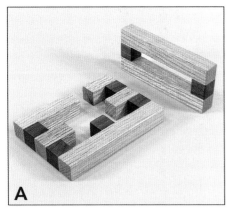  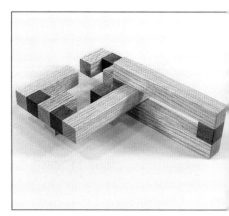

Starting with pieces 1 and 2, insert 1 into 2 and slide it to the right corner.

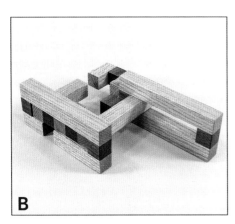 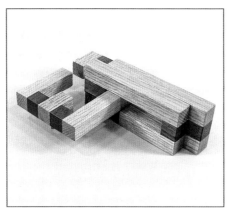

Add piece 3 by sliding it over piece 1 and back to the right corner, resting alongside piece 2.

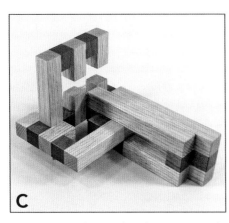 

Insert piece 4 into the slot in piece 1, and slide it into the same right corner, over piece 3.

**D**

ote the orientation of piece 5 and
sert it into the slot in piece 1.

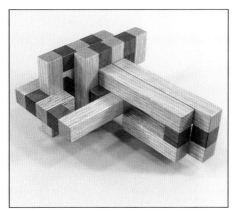

**E**

Slide piece 3 to the back, as it
passes through pieces 4 and 5.

**F**

ide piece 5 up one space.

**G**

Slide pieces 3 and 4 forward at the
same time.

**H**

Slide piece 4 to the right one space.

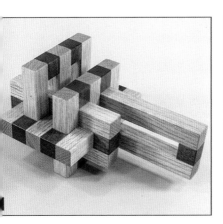

lide piece 4 forward one space,
ringing pieces 2 and 3 along.

**J**

Push piece 5 down into position and finish by sliding
piece 2 to the left.

# TWIN PENTOMINOES INTO A LIGHT BOX SOLUTION
*(instructions for building the puzzle are on p. 80)*

There are many ways to solve this puzzle. This solution requires many of the pieces to be inserted sequentially. The pieces get inserted from almost every angle, so showing the assembly with photos would be confusing. The instructions here describe the direction and order that each piece is inserted, and the accompanying diagram shows the orientation of each piece within the frame.

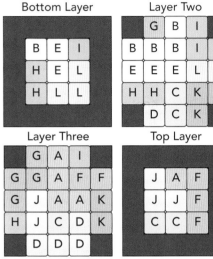

When inserting a piece into the box, be sure to compare its orientation to the diagram. You may not be able to rotate a piece into position after it is in the box. The pieces are inserted and slid into place without any rotation.

1. Begin by inserting piece B and nesting it into the left rear corner on the bottom layer.

2. Insert piece G and place it on top of B, filling the rear corner. You will have to move piece B out of the corner to fit piece G into place. Slide both pieces back into the corner.

3. Insert piece H through the top and slide it left, leaving just one opening through which you will slide E after inserting it through the bottom. The left window of the frame is now filled.

4. Insert piece I through the top and slide it to the right, then down, and then to the rear into the rear window.

5. Insert piece A through the top but not into its final position. Slide A toward the front, then to the left, where it will remain for a few moves.

6. Insert piece L through the right window and drop it into place, filling the bottom window.

7. Insert piece K through the front and slide it to the left, almost filling the right window.

8. Piece F goes in through the top and to the right, filling the right window completely.

9. Slide piece A to the right and to the rear, filling the rear window.

10. Drop piece C through the top, sliding it forward and to the righ but do not let it drop down into its final position. Insert piece J through the top, then slide it toward you, under C, and drop both pieces into position, filling the top window.

11. Place the last piece, D, through the front window, and your box filled.

Now see how many other solutions you can find to this puzzle.

# CAGED KNOT SOLUTION *(instructions for building the puzzle are on p. 86)*

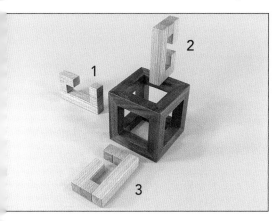

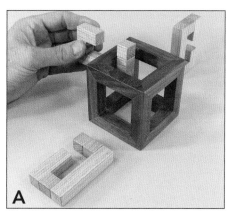

The Caged Knot has three pieces that are similar in shape and the "cage" or frame. Make note of the differences in the three pieces and their orientation.

Insert piece 1 through the back side and raise it up to the position shown.

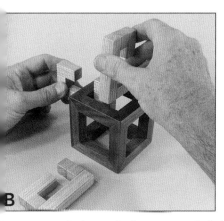

Drop piece 2 through the top, and slide piece 1 through the center hole.

Slide piece 3 in from the front and let it rest on the bottom of the cage.

Slide piece 2 to the right and centered in the cage, allowing it to drop down through the hole in piece 3.

Hold the cage and slide piece 3 up to the center of the cage, then pull it toward you.

*(continued on next page)*

# CAGED KNOT SOLUTION (continued)

Lift piece 2 up to be flush with the top of piece 1.

Slide piece 1 to the rear of the cage and then to the left of the cage.

Allow pieces 1 and 2 to drop down while keeping piece 3 in position.

Slide both pieces 1 and 2 forward to be centered within the frame.

Slide piece 1 forward to the center of the frame, followed by piece 2 sliding up, and finally, piece 3 sliding back to complete the Caged Knot.

ntify the pieces, which are num-
ered in order of assembly.

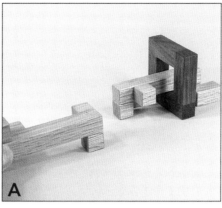

**A**

Insert piece 1 through the frame.
Note the correct orientation of
the piece.

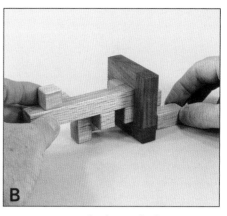

**B**

Insert piece 2, fit through the
L-shaped hole in the frame.

**C**

nce piece 2 is through the hole, slide it far enough past piece 1 that you
an slide it over the top of it as you slide piece 1 under and toward you.

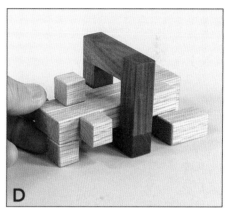

**D**

Allow piece 2 to drop and rest alongside piece 1.

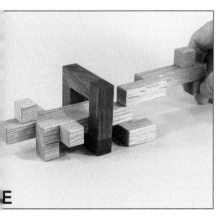

**E**

sert piece 3 from the right.

**F**

Push piece 3 through far enough that
you can slide it toward you, coming
to rest on top of piece 1.

*(continued on next page)*

# BUNDLE OF STICKS JR. SOLUTION *(continued)*

Grasp piece 2 and lift so that you can insert piece 4 under it.

The sticks have been bundled!

# MURBITER'S CUBE SOLUTION *(instructions for building the puzzle are on p. 96)*

*(instructions for building the puzzle are on p. 96)*

Here, we show two solutions: one for the Cube and one for the Brick. There are also a number of other unusual shapes that can be made from the eight identical pieces. Since all the pieces are the same, a pictorial assembly sequence will suffice.

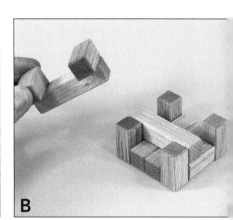

The Cube

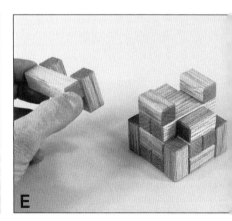

**G**

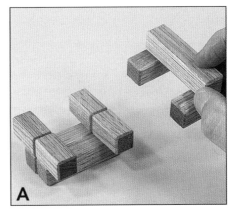

**A**

The Brick: Make two mirror-image assemblies as shown, and slide them together to begin to form the brick shape.

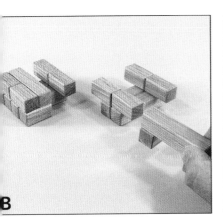

**B**

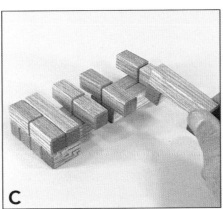

**C**

**D**

**E**

**F**

**G**

# TRIUMPH SOLUTION *(instructions for building the puzzle are on p. 99)*

The Triumph is a puzzle made from six identical pieces that can be assembled into more than one shape. Once you know the secret, assembly is relatively easy; however, it requires either large hands or the help of some tape or a rubber band. You assemble the puzzle in two halves and then slide the two halves together to complete the puzzle. Holding one half while assembling the other is the tricky part.

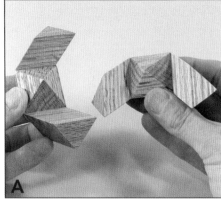

The six identical pieces.

Holding any two pieces as shown, align their center points.

Take another piece and lay it in the crook of the first two pieces. You have now created a sort of a pinwheel. Note the direction of the swirl of the pinwheel. Now create another assembly just like this one but with the swirl going in the opposite direction.

Here is where the rubber band or tape comes into play. Wrapping a rubber band around the trunk of your first assembly will enable you to make the second assembly more easily.

D

our two halves should look like this
when completed.

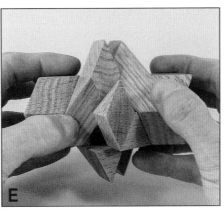

E

Align the two pinwheel assemblies
so that the fins of the pinwheels
alternate and bypass one another as
you slide the two together.

F

After removing the rubber band,
your Triumph should stand on
its own.

## The Star of David

You need to make only one
modification to the assembly
just completed to make an
entirely different shape.

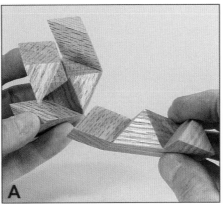

A

Holding one of the half assemblies, simply reverse the position of any one
of the pieces. This will create a pinwheel with one of the fins pointing
toward you.

B

Now make the mirrored half, revers-
ing one of the legs on this as well.

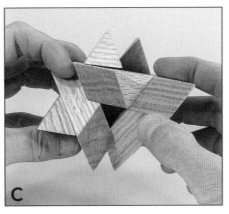

C

Slide the two halves together, and
make sure that the fins pointing out
are opposite one another.

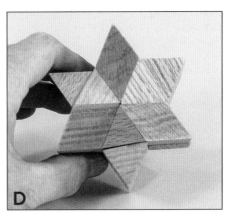

D

The end result is quite surprising and
very different from the first solution.

# VEGA SOLUTION *(instructions for building the puzzle are on p. 104)*

Like the Triumph, the Vega consists of six identical pieces and it goes together the same way, by making two half assemblies that are mirrors of each other and form a similar pinwheel effect.

Holding any two pieces, align their center points as shown.

Lay the third piece in the crook of the first two pieces to create your first pinwheel. As with the Triumph, you can use a rubber band to hold this assembly together.

When you have the two halves ready, make sure you have the swirls going in opposite directions. This is not as easy to see as it was with the Triumph.

The two pinwheel halves go together in the same manner as the Triumph. Alternate the fins so that they slide past one another as the two halves come together.

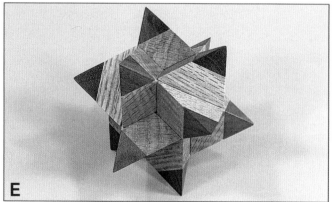

Viva Vega!

# DISTORTED CUBE SOLUTION *(instructions for building the puzzle are on p. 108)*

This puzzle gets its name because there are several variations of the solution that can fit into a box. However, it is difficult to get them to stand on their own without the box for support. My favorite solution is the one presented here, the Pyramid.

There are two (edge-beveled) 3-cube pieces and two 4-cube pieces. Close examination of the pieces shows that each of the 3-cube pieces simply had another cube added to it to make up the 4-cube pieces.

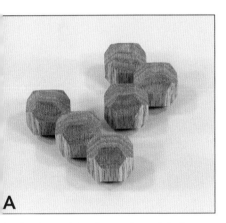

**A**

Beginning with pieces 1 and 2, lay them in the shape of a backward 4.

**B**

Take piece 3 and position it so that the extra cube (not part of the L) is pointing down.

**C**

Drop piece 3 into the space between the two existing pieces.

**D**

Lean piece 4 against the others, with one end forming the rest of the base and the other end topping off the pyramid.

**E**

The completed pyramid.

# OCTAHEDRAL CLUSTER SOLUTION *(instructions for building the puzzle are on p. 113)*

The Octahedral Cluster is another difficult puzzle to solve, even though it has only four pieces. Refer to the assembly map used to build the puzzle (see p. 113 ) to make sure you have the pieces oriented correctly.

The Octahedral Cluster goes together one way and only in the correct sequence as numbered here.

Position pieces 1 and 2 as shown. These two pieces must be carefully aligned to fit together. (If you glued up your pieces with the grain of the wood running in the same direction, this will help you align the pieces.)

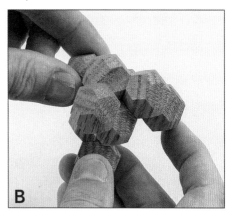

After fitting pieces 1 and 2 together, the assembly should appear as shown.

Piece 3 wraps around this assembly to complete the top half of the cluster.

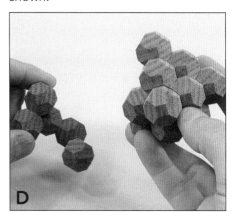

Hold piece 4 so that the four cubes make a U and one cube is sticking up.

Bring piece 4 upward to fit into the bottom of the assembly you are holding.

The completed cluster.

# PEG PILE SOLUTION (instructions for building the puzzle are on p. 118)

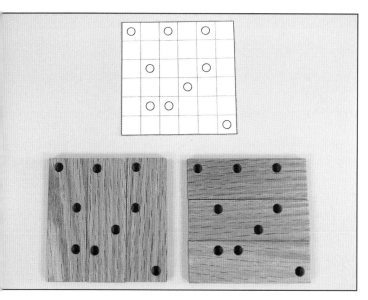

There is no secret to the Peg Pile other than memorizing the arrangement of the pieces. This is an extremely difficult puzzle to solve by trial and error. The solution is nothing more than looking at the pattern you used to drill the holes and aligning the sticks so that the holes correspond to the pattern. You may have to flip sticks back and forth until you have them all correctly aligned. Avoid showing the puzzle in its solved state to anyone for more than a few moments to avoid having the pattern memorized.

# CRUISER SOLUTION (instructions for building the puzzle are on p. 124)

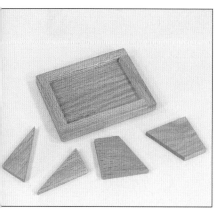

You should have a tray and two pairs of identical pieces.

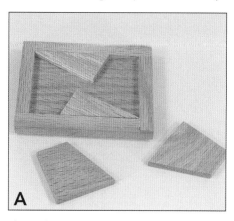

Place the two triangular pieces in the tray as shown.

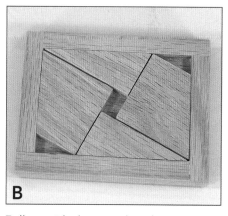

Follow with the two rhombic pieces. It seems so easy when you know the solution!

# TABULA CUBE SOLUTION *(instructions for building the puzzle are on p. 128)*

This is another puzzle where you may need to use rubber bands or tape to help with the assembly.

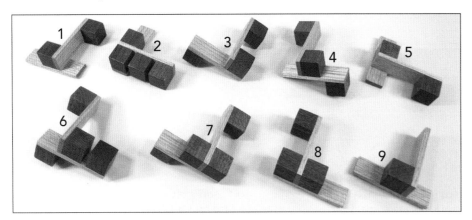

Identify the pieces, which are shown here in the order of assembly.

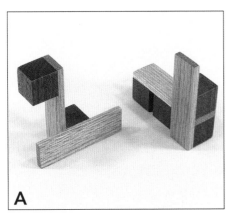

**A**

Slide piece 1 into piece 2. Note the orientation of piece 3.

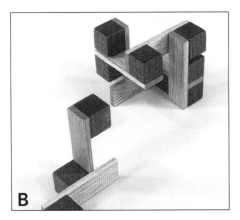

**B**

Place piece 3 on top of the assembly and hold it in position with tape or a rubber band. (You may be able to use your hands, but it gets much more difficult as you go along.)

**C**

Piece 4 slides under piece 3 and to the back of the cube. Lift the cube so that piece 4's top cube is resting on the horizontal crosspiece in the rear. Note the orientation of piece 5 (at top), which will be added next.

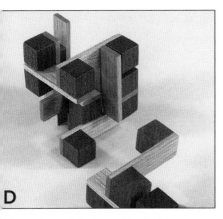

**D**

Bring piece 5 in from the left rear and let it sit with the bottom cube in the center of the assembly.

**E**

Insert piece 6 into the front, and slide it to the left one space. Notice the position of piece 7 (at top), which will be inserted into the top center of the assembly.

**F**

Insert piece 7; slide it forward one space and then down again one space. It should be resting just above the other pieces.

**G**

Insert piece 8 into the right side, lift it up one space, and slide it in one more space so that it is flush with the right side.

**H**

The piece on top (7) can now be pushed down into place.

**I**

Push the piece in front (6) flush with the front face.

**J**

Push in the left side piece (5) and push up the bottom piece (4).

**K**

Insert piece 9 into the space in the rear, locking everything in place.

# METRIC EQUIVALENTS

| Inches | Centimeters | Millimeters | Inches | Centimeters | Millimeters |
|---|---|---|---|---|---|
| 1/8 | 0.3 | 3 | 13 | 33.0 | 330 |
| 1/4 | 0.6 | 6 | 14 | 35.6 | 356 |
| 3/8 | 1.0 | 10 | 15 | 38.1 | 381 |
| 1/2 | 1.3 | 13 | 16 | 40.6 | 406 |
| 5/8 | 1.6 | 16 | 17 | 43.2 | 432 |
| 3/4 | 1.9 | 19 | 18 | 45.7 | 457 |
| 7/8 | 2.2 | 22 | 19 | 48.3 | 483 |
| 1 | 2.5 | 25 | 20 | 50.8 | 508 |
| 1 1/4 | 3.2 | 32 | 21 | 53.3 | 533 |
| 1 1/2 | 3.8 | 38 | 22 | 55.9 | 559 |
| 1 3/4 | 4.4 | 44 | 23 | 58.4 | 584 |
| 2 | 5.1 | 51 | 24 | 61.0 | 610 |
| 2 1/2 | 6.4 | 64 | 25 | 63.5 | 635 |
| 3 | 7.6 | 76 | 26 | 66.0 | 660 |
| 3 1/2 | 8.9 | 89 | 27 | 68.6 | 686 |
| 4 | 10.2 | 102 | 28 | 71.1 | 711 |
| 4 1/2 | 11.4 | 114 | 29 | 73.7 | 737 |
| 5 | 12.7 | 127 | 30 | 76.2 | 762 |
| 6 | 15.2 | 152 | 31 | 78.7 | 787 |
| 7 | 17.8 | 178 | 32 | 81.3 | 813 |
| 8 | 20.3 | 203 | 33 | 83.8 | 838 |
| 9 | 22.9 | 229 | 34 | 86.4 | 864 |
| 10 | 25.4 | 254 | 35 | 88.9 | 889 |
| 11 | 27.9 | 279 | 36 | 91.4 | 914 |
| 12 | 30.5 | 305 | | | |